James Baldwin's God

James Baldwin's God

sex, hope, and crisis in black holiness culture

Clarence E. Hardy III

The University of Tennessee Press
Knoxville

Library of Congress Cataloging-in-Publication Data

Hardy, Clarence E., 1970–
James Baldwin's god: sex, hope, and crisis
in Black holiness culture /
Clarence E. Hardy III.—1st ed.
p. cm.
Includes bibliographical references and index.
ISBN 1-57233-230-1 (cl.: alk. paper)
1. Baldwin, James, 1924–
—Religion.
2. Christianity and literature—
United States—History—
20th century.
3. Race—Religious aspects—
Holiness churches.
4. Sex—Religious aspects—
Holiness churches.
5. Holiness churches—United
States.
6. African Americans—Religion.
7. Religion in literature.
I. Title.
PS3552.A45 Z68 2003
818'.5409—dc21   2003006422

To Dawn Mays

my beloved wife and partner

Contents

Preface

hen I first read James Baldwin's *Go Tell It on the Mountain* as a college student, I was astonished to find my life in its pages. At that time, I was coming to terms with the religion of my youth and singing in a college choir that enabled me to claim the songs of Zion as my own for the first time. But that thin paperback from a used bookstore in town was a revelation of a different sort than the one I had long been seeking as I made the difficult transition to adulthood. In those yellowed pages I found the struggle I had with my church heritage represented in the words of another.

But beyond this moment of basic recognition, what I found most compelling about this very traditional coming-of-age story was the ambiguity of the protagonist's tenuous religious conversion. When I was younger, anxiety defined most of the time I spent thinking about God. Whenever a visiting evangelist came to my mother's church, I nearly always ran up to the altar at the earliest opportunity to get "right with God" and avoid what seemed to be the very real possibility of damnation. But no matter how earnestly or often I went, I never felt sure during those early years that I was really one of those who would be received by God when the world came to the fiery end promised in the countless sermons I heard. When, on occasion, I couldn't find my mother during the day, panic would overtake me. I would run around the house desperately calling her, hoping that she had not been caught up in the rapture, leaving me to face the horrors of God's capricious judgment alone. It was not until I left home that I gained any measure of assurance, but back then, despite the many moments I spent seeking a divine revelation at the foot of various altars, this deep-seated nervousness remained.

So when I read about John, Baldwin's protagonist and alter ego in that first novel, I resonated with his deep anxiety over his spiritual state. When I read John pleading just after his conversion with his friend Elisha never to forget that he was saved no matter what might happen and how far he might stray in the future, I knew—I understood—John's desperation. Just as he gains eternal salvation at the end of the novel, Johns feels the experience of divine revelation slipping from his grasp.

Baldwin's use of this disquiet to frame his novel not only highlights John's desperation but also depicts a black holiness culture that harshly restricts individuals' opportunity for growth. Even as he enters into this religious world of holiness culture, John is not sure he wants to be trapped in such a narrow, parochial tradition separated from the joyful pleasures and thrilling demands of the world. John's unease with God's ever-evasive but still-terrifying presence was Baldwin's inheritance and mine as well. And even though I largely made my peace with this religious culture that shaped my ambitions during my college years, something akin to John's ambivalence haunts me still. And so when I considered making a close examination of the evangelical impulse that animates so much of black religion in the United States, I knew that Baldwin would be a good partner in a critical appraisal of this religious tradition we both shared. I only had the slightest notion when I began of how demanding and uncompromising my chosen partner would be on this intellectual and spiritual journey. Even as Baldwin recognized the strength and power of black holiness tradition and its importance as a cultural marker for black identity in a hostile world, he also understood how compromised the religious culture of his upbringing was from its very inception.

His understanding of this compromised status was usually rendered in the autobiographical language and the personal terms he used so often. In one of his later extended essays, James Baldwin remembered how his stepfather, David Baldwin, a one-time Baptist minister, died because of his *"unreciprocated love for the Great God Almighty."*[1] This book, in fact, engages most directly that aspect of Baldwin's work that involves the substance and character of this unrequited love for a Christian god that is depicted as both silent before black suffering and as white—that is, actively opposed to the flourishing of black life. So, despite Baldwin's consistent portrayal of a black holiness culture full of energy and passionate life, there is an implicit criticism throughout his work that understands the principal backdrop to black people's conversion to Christianity in the United States to be shame and not hope.

This basic claim shapes the critical stance I adopt here, which attempts to examine the anatomy of a black evangelical consensus that dominated much of black religious expression from the establishment of institutional churches after the Civil War to Afro-Protestantism's waning influence after the black freedom movements of the 1960s. My approach here, however, not only tracks the limitations of a black evangelical tradition that emerges from compromised exilic beginnings, but also engages how many believers within this tradition hungered for divine judgment against the privileged who continued to hurt the weak. Baldwin's rhetoric invoked this strain within black evangelical tradition in his condemnation of those who in an attempt to maintain their social identity as white people would willfully deny their own moral connection (and biological kinship) to those of African descent, whom they continued to exploit. Baldwin inveighed with a nearly evangelical Christian fervor against the false innocence that he believed spurred this denial—which, Baldwin believed, was at the root of this nation's failure to grapple fully with racial and social injustice. Even as white Americans professed moral purity, they, in fact, in Baldwin's view, sullied themselves with how they enjoyed the fruits of privilege produced from the backs of black people.

But even as Baldwin relied on Christian rhetoric in his quest for social justice, his work, considered as a whole, suggests that while black evangelicalism embodies a posture of resistance against a hostile white world, its redemptive value ultimately fails to overcome the extent to which Christianity has contributed to African disfigurement. This complex relationship with Christianity is the core concern that animates my inquiry. My sincere hope is that this study will help not only to illuminate Baldwin's complex relationship but also to explore the anatomy of black holiness culture and the place it holds in black culture and black society.

Considering the Tragic Position of Black Religion: Interpretive Legacies and General Approaches

This work represents an exploration of Baldwin's serious moral purpose shaped and marked by sectarian black religious life even while it wrestles with the sharp limitations and contradictions of this religious heritage. Baldwin's peculiar relationship with black Christianity, and especially his rejection of it, in fact exposes the anatomy of a religious heritage in ways that have not been wrestled with sufficiently in the work of the contemporary black theological movement. So, for this current study Baldwin is important not just for how he was connected to black religious culture, but also for how he chose to disconnect himself from it. In the first instance, we learn paradoxically how strong and vibrant the tradition truly is from Baldwin's attempt to escape it. Despite his view that black religious expression harbored vengeful attitudes and illusory promises, he remained captive to its rhythms, language, and themes throughout his career. The religious world he often disdained actually animated his own moral rhetoric. Baldwin was forced, on occasion, to acknowledge that the religious fervor he saw as an adolescent was not simply an expression of repressed sexual tension but also a sign of irrepressible vigor and a dignified black humanity capable of confronting the greatest tragedies of life. As Baldwin acknowledges in his seminal *The Fire Next Time:* "In spite of everything, there was in the life I fled a zest and a joy and a capacity for facing and surviving disaster that are very moving and very rare."[2]

Baldwin's failure to disconnect entirely from what he saw as an insular holiness culture, however, may not just demonstrate the vigor of black holiness culture; it might also reveal how tragic the black exilic experience in the United

States truly is. While black religious culture clearly had true buoyancy that was attractive to Baldwin, the partial character of his rejection of the black evangelicalism suggests that Baldwin could not afford to turn away from these resources in his quest for human dignity. However compromised black religion may be, in a world as hostile to black life as this one is, black people within the United States must contend with the near genocidal reality of white supremacy with whatever resources are at hand. Few, if any, sources within black culture can offer unambiguous expressions of a healthy engagement with the broader dominant culture. And as Baldwin demonstrates so well, black religion is no different.

This project takes its initial cues from within the black theological movement of the late 1960s and the early to mid-1970s. The language and concerns of James Baldwin, especially as captured in *The Fire Next Time*, prefigure many of the early themes in the black theological movement as articulated by James Cone, William Jones, Charles Long, Gayraud Wilmore, and others. In this popular bestseller, Baldwin writes of his deep fascination with Malcolm X and the Nation of Islam and articulates a deep suspicion of white Christianity and ponders the possible malevolence of the Christian god toward black people. Both of these themes mirror the concerns and themes found in the early academic writings of the black theologians and scholars of religion that were shaped by the activism of the civil rights movement and the sensibilities of an ascending Black Power movement during the late 1960s. James Cone, the leading interpreter of the black theological movement, has confessed on more than one occasion that when he was learning to write forcefully he looked to the cadences and forms of Baldwin's essays as a model in his theological reflection. My work, however, most mirrors among these early pioneers the work of James's brother, Cecil Cone, who called into question the identity and allegiance of those inhabiting the academic environment as they attempted to express their relationship to the folk traditions that anchor black religious practice.[3] In so far as my work here seeks to grapple with the scandal of the evangelical impulse in much of black religion, it most reflects Cecil Cone's work among these early pioneers. Baldwin's rejection of the institutional forms of black Christianity, especially in its evangelical manifestations, provides perhaps a unique opportunity to explore the nature of black religion in the contemporary period outside the traditional boundaries of theological reflection.

The most immediate predecessor to this work is Theophus Smith, who labels his own noteworthy book, *Conjuring Culture*, a part of "the nascent field of African American spirituality." Smith situates his study between the "historical and social science study of religion on the one hand, and the black theology of liberation movement on the other, spanning literary aesthetic considerations in between."[4] I also find some inspiration in the recent work of Delores

Williams and the late Robert Hood in their use of an interdisciplinary cultural studies methodology.[5] This perspective is open to incorporating the insights of other disciplines outside of theology, including those methods associated with contemporary, literary scholarship in an effort to capture those "aesthetic considerations" that help shape the practice of black religion in the United States. Like that of Smith, my analysis will seek to be historically and anthropologically informed. But I also hope to be much more specific than he is in exploring how specific cultural practices represent the kind of conjuring culture Smith envisions. I will begin, in the first chapter, with perhaps what Baldwin felt was the most theatrical and compelling aspect of black religion: the initiation rite of conversion. Indeed, Baldwin's characterization and rejection of Christian conversion has significant implications for the larger symbolic world of black evangelicalism. My hope is that in unraveling Baldwin's reflections on the act of conversion as a specific, historical practice that has developed over time, I have expanded on Smith's approach and given texture to one of the ways black religion is actually conjuring culture in the contemporary period. This more critical approach will be able to keep track of Baldwin's challenge to the evangelical perspective and wrestle significantly with how the biblical influences within, and the supernatural folk sensibility of, black religion may both promote and restrict the possibilities for human freedom.

Within an interdisciplinary framework, conscious especially of the historical development of evangelicalism in both the white and black worlds of the United States, my point of departure is principally Baldwin's fiction and autobiographical essays. Baldwin's writing dramatizes for a worldwide audience the struggles he had with black religion. After I consider, in the first chapter, the performative aspects of black evangelical practice and the issues that bedevil any consideration of Baldwin's relationship to his religious heritage, I examine the nature and character of Baldwin's ultimate rejection of black Christianity in chapters 2 and 3. This rejection takes its initial shape in *Go Tell It* and his early short stories and then crystallizes most notably in his later fiction and essays, where he adopts a less sanguine view of his personal conversion experience. As Baldwin then begins to reckon with his own black body and his same-sex desires that this white Christian god appears to condemn, he begins to denounce this god more strongly over time, making the contradictions within black evangelicalism become much more stark and clear. The final sections of my book move away from Baldwin's criticism of church culture to how he employs its rhetoric in his cultural and political analysis of our notions of sex, the nature of American society, and the exilic character of black identity.

At its core, however, my study has some very basic limitations that almost all examinations of religious belief and practice share. Any examination of conversion experiences quickly becomes entangled with how to interpret religious experiences that are coupled with dreams, visions, and other states of consciousness that often accompany initiation rites. In her recent tour-de-force, *Fits, Trances, and Visions,* Ann Taves's exploration of how religious experiences in nineteenth-century American Protestantism, which were read through supernatural and naturalistic lenses, captures this problem of interpretation. As she cautions, the "experience of religion cannot be separated from the communities of discourse and practice that give rise to it *without becoming something else.*"[6] Taves addresses this problem through close historical analysis and careful descriptions of the dissociative states and religious practices she examines. Her analysis of these practices is marked by actual terms contemporaneous with the period in which they emerge. I engage this same problem initially with a strong focus on the initiation rite of evangelical conversion as a concrete, cultural practice anchored in the depth and complexity of Baldwin's own biography and his overall literary work as they relate to the history of his black holiness church heritage. From this perspective, I trace how this social practice connects to a broader symbolic evangelical world where the immediacy of sacred presence, one's personal confrontation with the texture and truth of biblical themes, and the sure reality of divine judgment all place a claim on the human imagination. This approach attempts to address the critics of Theophus Smith who question the absence of primary sources in his analysis of black spirituality as a conjuring culture.[7] I can only hope to deepen the discussion Smith has initiated. My approach here explores the limits and potential of the black holiness movement in the twentieth century as a specific expression of this conjuring culture mostly found in the urban environs of the United States as the principal carrier of the evangelical impulse in black religion. My work here as a fellow child of a conversion-brokered religion is meant as an exploration of sorts for what Baldwin's work might mean for the evangelical world he left behind, American identity, and the broader world of art, sex, and risk he lived and desperately sought after.

But I begin this exploration where Baldwin often began—with the theatricality of black religious practice and holiness culture. Baldwin's appreciation of the theatrics of religion competed fiercely with his disdain for what he perceived as its empty insularity. For Baldwin, religion, like the theater, conveys compelling stories from staged situations. The desire for dramatic truth rests on a certain falsity and a managed reality where audience members must shut out all intrusions from the outside to appreciate the world presented on stage. Baldwin, it seems, could appreciate the drama of the pulpit and the altar even as he took serious notice of the props on which religious theater always depended.

Acknowledgments

I did not complete this project alone. Caring family, colleagues, and mentors helped provide the emotional strength and the various tools I needed to begin this inquiry into the faith of my youth. Without them I would never have completed it. Whatever shortcomings remain exist because of my own limitations. To the extent that this project meets any of the goals I had for it simply demonstrates how wide and marvelous the support has been from so many.

I remain especially grateful to the late Rev. Dr. James M. Washington. He was the one who initially paved my way into Union Seminary more than ten years ago, and he was the person with whom I initially shared my thoughts about James Baldwin. His pastoral ministry and intellectual influence live on in the lives and work of many who study the genius of black religious traditions in the United States. I miss him still.

I am also extremely grateful for my doctoral committee and their insights and patience in what has become this book. Dr. David Leeming started me on my way early in 1996. He met with me in a Hungarian café across the street from St. John the Divine in the bustling intersection where Columbia University, the Upper West Side of New York, and Harlem meet. I will never forget how this newly retired professor, just freed from the strictures of university life, spent several hours with me, a new doctoral student. Our spirited discussion while we drank coffee and ate wonderful pastries that morning shapes my thinking on the work and life of James Baldwin to this day. I deeply appreciate his generous spirit. Dr. Delores Williams's sharp reading of my work on literary theory and black religion during my graduate studies and the audaciousness of her own interdisciplinary approach to black religion have been truly inspiring. I also thank Dr. Christopher Morse for his deeply pastoral presence and his never flagging concern for my welfare that bespeaks of basic yet deeply moving decency. And, of course, I am grateful for my adviser, Dr. James Cone, who has always had confidence in my ability to do the most serious of work. He has paved the way for a scholarship that is both rigorous and passionate about justice. I can only trust my work will meet his early confidence.

I remain thankful to the staff of Burke Library of Union Seminary, especially Caroline Bolden, who retrieved many sources for me through interlibrary loan. I also am deeply grateful to my church family of young adults at Convent

Avenue Baptist Church in Harlem, New York City, who accepted me both as a scholar and a minister. I was also very fortunate to have steadfast companions and critics along the way. I remain thankful for my colleagues Drs. Leslie Callahan and Sylvester Johnson and my brothers and comrades Adam Clark and Rafael Warnock at Union Seminary for their friendship during the journey. Dr. Dwight McBride, an early reader of this project, was immensely helpful in comments on my work. Joyce Harrison and the rest of the team at the University of Tennessee Press have honored me with their care and their confidence. I am also grateful for the anonymous reader who consistently challenged my work and was especially helpful in making initial revisions to the manuscript. I also thank Dr. Dale Irvin of New York Theological Seminary, who provided an extra boost of confidence right when I needed it. My colleagues at Rollins College in the Philosophy and Religion Department, Ms. Doris Lynn, Ms. Lynda Murphy, and Drs. Hoyt Edge, Tom Cook, Yudit Greenberg, Scott Rubarth, and Margaret McLaren all provided me space and encouragement to finish what I had started in New York during my first year of teaching. I only hope I can repay their generosity of spirit.

I remain indebted to the James Baldwin Estate, which has graciously established an arrangement with me to reprint excerpts from James Baldwin's *The Fire Next Time* (copyright © 1962, 1963 by James Baldwin. Copyright renewed. Published by Vintage Books) and *Blues for Mister Charlie* (copyright © 1964 by James Baldwin. Copyright renewed. Published by Vintage Books). I am also indebted to Doubleday, a division of Random House, for granting me permission to publish excerpts from Baldwin's *Go Tell It on the Mountain* (copyright 1952, 1953 by James Baldwin). I am grateful to Beacon Press, Boston, for granting permission to reprint excerpts from Baldwin's *Notes of a Native Son* (copyright © 1955, renewed 1983 by James Baldwin).

Most of all, I am grateful for the family that has nurtured me from the beginning and suffered through my doubts and anxieties. My mother, Mae Alice Brewer Hardy, taught me what it meant to be a Christian, and my father, Clarence Hardy Jr., taught me what it meant to be a man responsible to his family and his community. My daughter, LaRae Joelle, was a constant joy and gave me times of play and respite from the rigors of writing and editing. My loving wife, Rev. Dawn Mays, is the most responsible for the completion of this text. Molded by her late father, Larkey Mays, and her mother, Cornelia Bennett Mays, my wife is a true warrior for justice and tenderness. Her steadfast love and prayers sustained me despite my doubts. And even when she did not entirely understand her anxious husband, she remained always strong in her confidence that what had been begun would be completed. It is to her, my heart and my beloved, that I dedicate this work.

Chapter 1

"But the City Was Real"

religion as bloodless theater

They [my old childhood friends] still believed in the Lord, but I had quarreled with Him, and offended Him, and walked out of His house.

No Name in the Street, *1972*

Born on August 2, 1924, at Harlem Hospital across the street from the library he would almost daily inhabit as a youth, the future boy preacher would become one of the most celebrated writers the United States produced during the twentieth century. But, at the close of his days in France, where he had spent the bulk of his exile from the country of his birth, Baldwin confessed to David Leeming, a close friend and one of his later biographers, that if he had it to do all over again, he would have been a playwright and perhaps an actor rather than the novelist and incendiary essayist he had become. So, although a sexy Parisian novel and an explosive essay and polemic on race had catapulted Baldwin during the 1960s onto the national stage and garnered him the international attention he seemed to crave, it was the theater that had captured his remaining energies in southern France. It was his last unpublished work, *The Welcome Table,* that occupied his attention and kept him working just months before his death. This play, in a way, represented the culmination of his longtime fascination with the theater.[1]

Beginning, indeed, with *The Amen Corner,* written in the early 1950s, Baldwin continued to work sporadically at playwriting throughout his career, even though his editors always wanted him to return to the novels and essays that had first cemented his reputation as a writer. Even though his two published plays questioned the parochialism of church culture, his plays also, perhaps most directly, reflected and celebrated the rhythms of black religious life. They displayed a concern with religion that permeated Baldwin's entire work and perhaps most clearly revealed his textured and often troubled relationship with the black holiness culture that so shaped his tumultuous adolescence and his later career.

An early poem of Baldwin's, "Black Girl Shouting," was written for his high school magazine, *Magpie,* and demonstrates that from the very beginning his connection to the rhythms of black religious life would inform nearly all of his work. The young Baldwin begins with a phrase percolating with black vernacular speech patterns he must have heard as a boy. With the first couplet — "stomp my feet / An' clap my han's" — Baldwin recounts a young girl's "shout" and intermeshes her moment of religious ecstasy with the rhythmic pulses of the clapping hands and feet of a nameless congregation that spurs her on. This early poem prefigures the role religion would have in Baldwin's plays. Immersed in this early verse we can almost anticipate how important his own religious conversion would be in shaping his later published work; we can already see him struggling against a deeply insular, though lively, holiness church culture.

Though still a believer and active preacher, Baldwin expresses in this early poem all the ambiguity and doubt at the heart of his hunger for religious faith. From the first couplet to the later stanzas, Baldwin invokes the rhythms of the church while establishing through his descriptions of this young girl's "shout" how pain informs moments of genuine religious fervor and frames black experience in the United States. As Baldwin writes,

> Black girl, whirl
> Your torn, red dress
> Black girl, hide
> Your bitterness
>
> Black girl, stretch
> Your mouth so wide
> None will guess
> The way he died[2]

In this description of the young girl's religious ecstasy, Baldwin mingles images of her exultant shouts of worship with those of Christ's crucifixion even as he hints of the "bitter" grind of her daily existence as a black person in the United States. The tension between these two realities of joy and pain captures the tortuous relationship to the vibrant religious practices and beliefs of the church that his novels and essays would later explore in deeper detail.

In later essays, long after he would leave the church behind, Baldwin describes his own traumatic conversion as a fourteen-year-old in *The Fire Next Time* as inexplicably linked to the first flowering of his adolescence and the beginnings of a fiercely felt sexual awakening. Indeed, he confesses quite suggestively that his conversion was like "surrendering" to a "spiritual seduction." But since this surrender came long before what he euphemistically calls "any carnal knowledge," it overwhelmed him in ways that he could not understand because he did not yet know the pleasures of sex.[3] Baldwin ultimately rejected the soundness of this conversion event because its principal drive was escapist; it wrongly provided an escape from his intensely felt sexual desires and a place of refuge from a dangerous world. Long before he had the courage to leave the church, however, Baldwin believed that the insular church culture of his boyhood was fundamentally divorced from a life of physical love and art. Recalling the torment he experienced in the "lie" of the pulpit more than a decade after *Fire,* Baldwin describes how a classmate and friend advised him not to preach what he no longer believed and to leave the bounds of the institutional church. To stay would be, in his friend's estimation, a "desperate" act of "cowardice."[4] And so, spurred by his friends, Baldwin admits in a later essay that he "abandoned the ministry" so that he would not "betray" himself.[5]

Baldwin's description of his final rejection of a church, which had so captured his personality and shaped his ambitions for three years, mirrors the anthropological work of Victor Turner and other scholars who have linked the life and form of the stage with religious ritual.[6] Baldwin tells us in his extended essay on movies, *The Devil Finds Work,* about the moment of inspiration when he initially made the connection between theatrical and religious performance. At first when he joined the church he had assumed that his love and participation in the theater was over. Baldwin confesses in this essay that it took "a while" to realize that he had in fact never left the theater—that in fact he was actually "working in one."[7] And while trumpeting his playwriting prowess in introductory notes for his first play, *The Amen Corner,* Baldwin also makes this connection between the theater and religion. As Baldwin writes: "I knew, in attempting to write the play, by the fact that I was born in the church. I knew that out of the ritual of the church, historically speaking, comes the act of the theatre, the *communion* which is the theater."[8]

This connection between the stage and religious drama was long-standing for Baldwin. During the 1930s in New York City, Orilla Miller, his sixth-grade teacher in Public School 24, saw promise in the young Baldwin and took him to see movies and plays. One play that made a strong impression on the eleven-year-old boy was a production of *Macbeth* by Orson Welles for a WPA theater group in Harlem with an all-black cast. It was a revelation to Baldwin. In an interview several decades later with a Baldwin biographer, Miller recalled how the young Jimmy was silent and "entranced" throughout the entire production.[9] In his own writings, Baldwin remembers how struck he was with the actual physical presence of black actors and the curious mixture of the "real and the imagined" that comprises the essence of the theater.[10] In the moments right before he falls under the power of the Spirit in Mother Rosa Horn's Pentecostal church, the memories of this *Macbeth* are the thoughts that occupy his mind. And Baldwin did not believe that it was accidental that he was "carrying around the plot of a play" in his head when he suddenly found himself on the church floor "crying holy unto the Lord."[11]

Baldwin always thought he could have been "a great actor" because the theater and the religious drama of the church come from "the same forces, the same nerves," and they both depended on "maverick freak poets and visionaries" like him for their life. Baldwin sees the drama of the stage and the pulpit as profoundly human creations expressive of a "need" and "impulse more mysterious than our desire."[12] But in the comparison between the two found in *The Devil Finds Work*, the church is the endeavor found wanting. While theater is created in the tension between the "real and the imagined," Baldwin cautions that theater should never deny the real lest it become like the church. It cannot rest "in the presence of shadows" because it is the response "to one's flesh and blood" that becomes the very vehicle for self and collective transformation. As Baldwin writes, "we are *all* each other's flesh and blood. This is a truth which it is very difficult for the theater to deny, and when it attempts to do so the same thing happens to the theater as happens to the church; it becomes sterile and irrelevant, a blasphemy, and the true believer goes elsewhere—carrying, as it happens, the church and the theater with him."[13] In the face of his hunger for the power and immediacy that comes from the stage, Baldwin finds the theatrics of religion strangely sterile. The way, indeed, Baldwin characterizes the lack of substance inherent in religion's drama demonstrates perhaps best of all the peculiar relationship he had throughout his life with Christianity.

This relationship began with his parents, who exposed the young Baldwin to Christian teaching and practice. Although his stepfather, David Baldwin—whose family name he adopted—initially reared him in the Baptist faith, the young Baldwin did not truly surrender to the power of religious ritual until his teenage years.[14] When he did succumb during the summer of his fourteenth birthday, it happened when he was caught by the presence of the South Carolina–born dressmaker-turned-Pentecostal preacher, Rosa Artimas Horn. So even though his father, who had been an itinerant minister from New Orleans, sometimes took him as a boy to Adam Clayton Powell's well-regarded Abyssinian Baptist Church, the young Jimmy Baldwin was first truly initiated into the fellowship of believers at the sanctified church Horn founded in 1926. It was there, at the Mount Calvary Assembly Hall of the Pentecostal Faith Church for All Nations, that the precocious young writer was overcome with what he describes as "the strangest sensation I have ever had in my life." One moment Baldwin was clapping and singing along with everyone else, and in the next he suddenly found himself flat on his back with the "lights beating down" on his face, surrounded by "vertical saints." These saints circled round him, just as the windows carrying the message "Jesus Saves" in several languages circled the outside panels of the church building.[15]

Mother Horn (as her devoted followers and foes alike called her) headed a dynamic ministry in Harlem. Her church of three thousand actively fed thousands more during the depression years even as the organization spread into five cities along the eastern seaboard by 1934, several years before Baldwin's conversion experience. Located above the dance club she would continue to battle with for many years, Horn, through her church, vigorously campaigned against the many pool halls and other night establishments that dotted Harlem's urban landscape. Her exploits filled the local black papers even as her early radio addresses, widely heard on Sunday and Wednesday nights, gained popularity and sparked a lively rivalry with Father Divine, who then tried to run her out of town because her following competed with his own. She stands out as a woman preacher in the 1930s and 1940s who proudly proclaimed her right to preach despite the male naysayers of her day. It is of little surprise that Baldwin found in her a dramatic flare that would provide the basis for the lead character, Margaret, in his first staged play, *The Amen Corner*.[16]

As Margaret is for her followers in the play, Horn was magnetic for the young Baldwin. Years later Baldwin would describe her as an "extremely proud and handsome woman," with a regal bearing carrying the mixed heritage of Africa, Europe, and the American Indian stamped on her facial features. Her inviting presence reminded Baldwin of how various street hustlers seduced their human prey for sex and other games on the always-busy city corners. At their first meeting, orchestrated by his boyhood friend Arthur Moore, Horn stunned the young Jimmy with a question that echoed the invitations "pimps and racketeers" had offered him before. When Horn asked, "Whose little boy are you?" Baldwin, on this occasion, did not countenance a refusal. "My heart replied at once," Baldwin tells us in *Fire*, "Why yours." And so while he had usually refused the street racket in the past, when Horn offered a chance to join a "church racket" Baldwin gladly accepted.[17] And even as Baldwin got his start as a preacher in another Pentecostal church shortly after his conversion, it was Horn's example it seems that initially shaped his creative imagination and would later augment his sense of a link between the rituals of religion and of theater.

When Baldwin left the church for the last time and finally acted on his rejection of any tangible belief in God, he tiptoed away from the sanctuary during a Sunday sermon just in time to go to an early matinee with a young friend. Looking back on his experience as a boy preacher, Baldwin describes his talent for words and religious exhortation as a "gimmick."[18] This was not entirely a negative characterization of religion. With this language, Baldwin sought to describe religious activity as similar to other human endeavors, both criminal and virtuous, that allowed young black people an opportunity to lift themselves out of the perilous circumstances they lived in. Everyone needed a gimmick, and Baldwin would probably have conceded that the art, fiction, and essays he would later pursue were also gimmicks of a kind. For Baldwin, religious people were different, however, with how obsessed they were with safety and how earnestly they seemed to avoid risk.

As we have seen, Baldwin's musings on the theater demonstrates how complicated his relationship with his religious heritage could be. In his comparisons of Christian rituals to aspects of actual stagecraft, Baldwin depicts religion as bloodless theater, cut off from reality in its attempts to serve as a refuge for the meek from a combustible and secular world pulsing with danger. As a minister, Baldwin clearly saw the theatrical elements of religion and knew how they worked. He writes in *Fire:* "Being in the pulpit was like being in the theatre; I was behind the scenes and knew how the illusion was worked."[19] But when he left the church, Baldwin became a "sinner," like Esther, a character in his first novel, *Go Tell It on the Mountain,* who knows that religious theatrics while entertaining will ultimately come to nothing. Baldwin in one early church scene describes Esther as a sexually adventurous woman who everyone assumed would never become a formal member of a Christian community. But when she goes to church to spy on the minister who wants to bed her, she enjoys its theatrics and revels in its impossible promises. At the back of the church she sits and looks about "with a bright pleased interest, as though she were at a theater and were waiting to see what improbable delights would next be offered her."[20] And when Baldwin himself leaves the church and steps outside the religious world he once so completely inhabited, he sees as Esther does. The promises of eternal delight that seemed so real before from within the walls of the church are revealed to be the empty theatrics they always were.

Reading and writing for Baldwin, however, had everything to do with the real and concrete world around him. These literary activities represented Baldwin's best effort to embrace with integrity the broader world beyond the bloodless theater of religion. As his faith began to slip away, his religion became a fortress in his imagination that seemed specifically designed to ward off the dangers of the vast, outside world writing and art brought to him. Not surprisingly, as his ambitions for reading and writing increased, his allegiance to the faith he preached diminished. In *Fire,* Baldwin explains that his loss of faith was gradual and diminished almost "imperceptibly." Even so he could still date the "slow crumbling of my faith, the pulverization of my fortress," to the year after he started preaching, "when," in his words, he "began to read again."[21] His interest in the written word and literary imagination became his new calling and pushed him not so gently out of the world revealed in the biblical stories and rhythmic words of worship and song toward an outside world filled with sinful pleasures. His drive for ministry was replaced with what Baldwin often said was his greatest ambition: "to be an honest man . . . [and] a good writer."[22]

His observations of a church built on bloodless theatrics and gimmickry emerge principally in his essays of the 1960s and 1970s. But these later views take form relatively early in his career as a published writer. In *Go Tell* and his early play, *The Amen Corner,* the church is depicted as a repository of illusions that attempts but fails to ward off the possibilities of human secular activity and pleasures. The young John Grimes, early in Baldwin's first novel, surely mirrors Baldwin's own life when he looks down from the top of a large hill in the middle of Central Park, sees the urban bustle and the gleaming buildings below, and faces the temptations only the city can offer. Despite the danger the city's rich white inhabitants represent, standing astride their environment and exploiting and dominating all who fall outside their own kin, the city, with its vibrancy and its worldly pleasures and artistic delights, overwhelms any dreams of heaven and any yearning for the possibilities of divine retribution. "To hurl away, for a moment of ease, the glories of eternity!" Baldwin exults within the spirit of his protagonist. "These glories were unimaginable," he cautions, "but the city was real."[23] Beside the vibrant reality and concrete temptations of modern urban life, the illusory promises of a glorious afterlife lose their sparkle and allure. Although Baldwin seems continually caught throughout his career between intensely religious and secular worlds, he squarely faces the secular—he always faces the city.

Indeed, although Baldwin continues throughout his fiction and essays to represent religion as an alluring tapestry of images and symbols, he also suggests that few who actually embrace its promises of eternity fully believe its concrete reality enough to die for it. In comparing those who claimed to want true integration of the South during the 1950s and early 1960s with believers who always accent their ordinary speech with the joys of eternity, Baldwin bemoans in his essay "A Fly in Buttermilk" that "the future is like heaven—everyone exalts it but no one wants to go there [right] now."[24] But even before Baldwin published his first novel, in an essay written for *Harper's Magazine* in 1949, he renders his verdict on religion in stark terms as he criticizes Richard Wright's *Native Son* and his tragic literary creation—the black murderer and protagonist Bigger Thomas. "Bigger's tragedy," Baldwin writes, "is not that he is cold or black or angry, not even that he is American, black; but that he has accepted a theology that denies him life."[25]

And yet, even though he suggests that the sanctified churches of his youth contravene life, their culture is one that also expresses life's passions. Baldwin acknowledges in *Fire:*

> There is no music like that music, no drama like the drama of the saints rejoicing, the sinners moaning, the tambourines racing, and all those voices coming together and crying holy unto the Lord. There is still, for me, moreover, there is no pathos quite like the pathos of those multicolored, worn, somehow triumphant and transfigured faces, speaking from the depths of a visible, tangible, continuing despair of the goodness of the Lord.[26]

With his vigorous language, Baldwin makes clear how despite its seemingly empty theatrics and insularity the church still managed through its rhetoric, rhythm, and song to capture his personality and shape his hopes and ambitions for three years as a young minister; the church, it seemed, was the very vehicle for life's vibrancy. And even after he renounced the church, Baldwin found that its rhetoric and sensibility continued to have an extensive impact on his self-definition and the ways he chose to express his moral commitments. It had, indeed, provided him with an "inner vocabulary" that he would use to express his hopes for love and his passion for social and economic justice throughout his public life.[27] And Baldwin was brash enough to use the very teachings of the church's founder against its rigid organizational structure and against its often-callous disregard for the most marginal in the human family. When Baldwin pressed for equity for persons caught on the very margins of society, this Christian-derived commitment became the platform for his criticisms against Christian institutions. He condemned them most for their exclusivity and their lack of empathy for the very outsiders with whom Jesus often associated.

But even as he knew the church to be repressive and insular, Baldwin continued to feel connected to the church. Years after he left the church as a boy preacher, Baldwin continued to bring Europeans and white American editors and friends to Mother Horn's church when he was in New York so that they could experience the vitality and energy of black religious life for themselves.[28] As Baldwin admitted to the renowned anthropologist Margaret Mead in a published dialogue between the two: "The whole question . . . of religion has always really obsessed me."[29] He knew that what he called his "adolescent holy-roller terrors" would mark him forever.[30] And as Michael Lynch, long concerned with the themes of religion in Baldwin's work, describes Baldwin's relationship with the god of his evangelical youth: "Baldwin's work evinces a writer 'afflicted' with belief in God as an unshakable burden."[31] In a modern world in which much of the philosophical apparatus supporting religious belief has collapsed, religion has often been experienced as a burdensome compulsion that separates the physical body from the psychological self, even as it animates persons in their struggle for self-expression and identity. For many this ambiguous relationship to religious belief and practice is all that remains of their theistic aspirations. In this context, Baldwin's own complicated relationship with religion and the Christian god was truly a modern one.

Interpreting Baldwin's Relationship with Christian Faith

Even though Baldwin's relationship with Christian faith, marked with strain and some confusion, links him with how many moderns still relate to religious traditions, its ambiguity presents the deepest methodological problems in interpreting the meaning(s) of Baldwin's connection to holiness culture. The difficulties begin with Baldwin's attempt to see black Christianity as distinctive and separate from the Christianity white Americans and Europeans practiced. Even though he acknowledges in one late essay that the church he came from and "the church to which most white Americans belong" have both been called Christian, he insists that they are in fact vastly different. Speaking of white and black Americans, Baldwin explains that they do not share "the same hope or speak the same language." These differences, according to Baldwin, are due in part to "pragmatic decisions concerning Property made by a Christian State sometime ago."[32] For Baldwin, when the church aligned itself in 314 C.E. with imperialist power and the Roman emperor, avarice and the desire for power then helped to define and shape a Christianity that was different from the religion Jesus demonstrated. This change, Baldwin suggests, would later allow for the differences between white and black Christianity that would emerge in the United States. In addition, for Baldwin the spirituals and the blues, which emerged from a long history of profound black suffering and a polytheistic past, serve as significant cultural markers that distinguish Afro-Protestantism from the rest of American Christianity. As Baldwin says in a speech before the World Council of Churches (WCC): "The blues are a historical creation produced by the confrontation precisely between . . . the black pagan from Africa, and the alabaster cross."[33]

Even as Baldwin maintains these significant distinctions, his general critical stance against the insularity of religion undermines, to some degree, his attempt to valorize black religion as separate from the dominant modes of imperialist Christianity in the West. "Because I was born in a Christian culture," Baldwin says in that same WCC speech, "I never considered myself to be totally a free human being."[34] And this statement belies his claims that black and white Christianity are materially different in ways that matter. That he was raised as a black Christian familiar with the rhythms of the blues did not seem to make much difference; he was still not, in his words, "the totally free human being" he wished to be.

The professional critical response to Baldwin's first novel, *Go Tell It*, however, illustrates the most profound methodological hurdles in any assessment of the strained relationship Baldwin had with his Christian upbringing. Barbara K. Olson, in a recent article, notes how critics have been spilt over whether the novel as a whole is "an ironic indictment of Christianity" or a "a stirring vindication." Critics' assessments pivot to some degree on how they understand John Grimes's conversion at the end of the novel. Like any initiation rite, conversion can be seen as the entrance of a new member into an adult community, with all the status that it implies, or as an opportunity for a broader group to exercise social control on its individual members. Surely, elements of both exist, but Olson's question about the nature of Grimes's conversion is still quite pertinent. In her words, is John's conversion at the end of the novel an example of his "subjugation to the group or integration into it?"[35] Some point to the sunny tone that ends Baldwin's first novel that suggests the possibility of transformation as the young protagonist John Grimes appears to escape from underneath the authority of his repressive father. In this view, John becomes, through his conversion on the threshing floor, a genuine adult member of the community. Indeed, John's uplifting statement that concludes the novel suggests a satisfaction that can only come with a boy's graduation into manhood. "I'm ready," he says, "I'm coming. I'm on my way."[36] Others, taking note of how Baldwin linked his conversion to adolescent sexual frustration and his "forbidden" desires for men, see John's conversion as "subjugation" and "a disheartening defeat in which he recapitulates his forbearers' [*sic*] experience."[37]

Olson is quite persuasive when she notes how ambiguously Baldwin treats John's conversion in *Go Tell It* when read without knowledge of Baldwin's comments in *Fire*, published nearly a decade later. In Olson's reading, Baldwin's play *The Amen Corner*, written just after *Go Tell It*, is his attempt to mount a clearer indictment of the church culture he himself rejected in the course of his own maturation to adulthood.[38] Indeed, in the play the young Baldwin-like character, David Alexander, soundly rejects the church in order to embrace the outside world, while John in *Go Tell It* is incorporated, however ambiguously, within the religious community. The pastor of the church and David's mother, Margaret Alexander, modeled on Mother Horn and under whom Baldwin himself was converted, is depicted as callously abandoning her husband, her son, and love itself for a ministry based on her thirst for power. Baldwin explains Margaret's dilemma in the notes that preface his published play: "She [Margaret] is in the church because her society has left her no other place to go. Her sense of reality is dictated by the society's assumption, which also becomes her own, of her inferiority. Her need for human affirmation, and also for vengeance, expresses itself in her merciless piety."[39] It is only at the end of the play when Margaret has lost everything—her son, her husband, and her ministry—that she realizes that "loving the Lord" is not found in the rituals of the church. It is found instead in loving everyone—both the high and the low—whether they are church members or not.

But despite how harshly Baldwin depicts Margaret and her religious beliefs, most who saw *The Amen Corner*, including the strongest critics of the play, were still, in the words of one critic, caught up in the "rhythms of the Afro-American church." They derived a more favorable impression of the dignity and vitality of churchgoers than the actual written words of the play would seem to suggest with their strong indictment of a loveless church.[40] Indeed, Baldwin intended that audiences identify, despite themselves, with the congregation represented in the play. Baldwin wanted playgoers to experience what he did when he was converted; he wanted them to recognize their own potential to be caught up in an emotionally charged world as he was as a young believer and minister. "I knew that what I wanted to do in the theatre," Baldwin writes, "was to recreate moments I remembered as a boy preacher, to involve the people, even against their will, to shake them up, and hopefully to change them."[41]

A final judgment, of course, on whether *Go Tell It* or Baldwin's work as a whole ultimately affirms or indicts holiness church culture and Christianity is probably not possible. Even so, there has been a gradual evolution in how literary critics have judged the role and status of religion in Baldwin's work. When they first began to assess Baldwin's work many scholars largely ignored the role of religion in it. During the late 1960s, Nathan Scott, a theologian and literary specialist, saw only "the memory of Christianity" in *Go Tell It*.[42] By the mid-1970s, many critics, noting the extensive use of religious imagery throughout his literary career, either celebrated its presence or simply pronounced Baldwin a secular preacher of love and justice—turning elements of his novels and even his autobiographical essays into slogans for theologians and religious thinkers of all stripes.[43]

The difficulty with this more contemporary view is that Baldwin very rarely engaged Christian doctrine. What Baldwin did instead was describe and criticize general tendencies within Christian institutions. He was rarely specific, however, about how Christian beliefs might have shaped institutional and individual religious practice. Assuredly, Baldwin's reproach of established church institutions and his strong moral critique of Christianity's corrupt connection to imperialist state power, anticipates, in great measure, the approach of many liberation theologians in the contemporary period. Shaped by the various people's movements for social change during the 1960s and 1970s, these theologians were convinced that the struggle for social justice was intrinsic to real religious commitment. Baldwin made this same connection and on this central issue of social justice attains a certain degree of specificity in his rhetoric and passion. When the famous anthropologist Margaret Mead forces Baldwin to acknowledge the role Christianity had in his own moral rhetoric, Baldwin, under pressure in a recorded conversation published in the early 1970s concedes her point. But he then protests:

> But what Christians seem not to do is identify themselves with the man they call their Savior, who, after all, was a very disreputable person when he was alive and who was put to death by Rome, helped along by the Jews in power under Rome . . . . So, in my case, in order to become a moral human being . . . I have to hang out with publicans and sinners, whores and junkies, and stay out of the temple where they told us nothing but lies anyway.[44]

Most contemporary liberation theologians share Baldwin's attachment to this historical Jesus strongly associated with the marginal and the outcast. But despite this mutual regard for a Jesus linked with the dispossessed, it is Baldwin's unstinting commitment to freedom and his willingness to subordinate his artistic talents in the struggle for social justice and not any specific Christian teaching that most connects Baldwin to contemporary liberation theologians. Many critics have chastised Baldwin's apparent willingness in his later work to compromise the aesthetic demands of fiction for the sake of protest. They see some irony in Baldwin's later stance because this Harlem-born writer first caught the attention of the liberal New York literary establishment with his pointed criticism of Richard Wright for subsuming the full expression of black life in the production of one-dimensional protest literature. Undaunted by such criticism, Baldwin acknowledged in several interviews and conversations that he felt "an enormous sense of responsibility" as a well-known black writer. And indeed, especially during the civil rights struggle of the 1960s and thereafter, Baldwin increasingly related his artistic work to his active political engagements. As Baldwin told one interviewer, John Hall, in 1970: "What is important about my work, which I realized when I was a little boy, partly from the Church perhaps . . . is that nothing belongs to you. My talent does not belong to me." His talent, Baldwin continued, is "important only insofar as it can work toward the liberation of other people."[45]

But beyond this concern for social justice, Baldwin raised other issues in his early novels and essays that prefigured the fascinations of the first large group of academically trained black theologians writing in the late 1960s and throughout the 1970s. Issues like the significance of self-hatred in black life, the rising importance of black nationalism, and probing questions about God's existence in the face of the seeming permanence of black suffering all haunt Baldwin's *Fire*. And these same issues shaped some of the liveliest early debates within the black theological movement of the early 1970s.[46] But one of the few issues of traditional doctrine Baldwin did dare to engage directly was the identity of Christ. Baldwin would consistently challenge the reputed uniqueness of Jesus and the nature of salvation in ways that mirror the religious perspectives among contemporary feminist and gay and lesbian theologians. "He [Jesus] claimed to be the Son of God," Baldwin said before the WCC. "That claim was a revelation and a revolution because it means that we are all the sons of God." For Baldwin, being sons (and presumably daughters also) meant that each person was responsible for their own salvation and each had the ability, in his words, "to expand and transform God's nature."[47] Both of these claims are deeply resonant with the project of many contemporary feminist and gay theologians. Many in recent years have consistently challenged the exclusive and the reputedly unique character and status of Jesus that traditional church doctrine proclaims.[48]

To the extent Baldwin maintains any allegiance to Christianity, despite his ultimate rejection of organized Christian faith and theism, he does offer a prophetic vision for the church. His thirst for freedom and his deep concern for the downtrodden in society certainly continue to call the church and all moral people inside and outside of religious communities into account. Most literary critics, however, have ignored Baldwin's religious heritage. They have discounted it as simply something Baldwin was trying to get rid of as he settled into a new humanist consciousness without religious belief and a Christianity he largely left behind.[49] But those critics who have attempted to treat Baldwin's religious heritage seriously have neglected to account fully for how Baldwin ultimately rejects Christianity and its god. Patricia Schnapp in her dissertation that characterizes Baldwin as a liberation theologian represents this perspective well. As she writes: "Baldwin has never had any argument with the gospel as such. What he has criticized is rather, institutionalized Christianity as embodied in the churches and the failure of nominal Christians to live up to the moral tenets of their religion."[50]

But any effort that aims to domesticate Baldwin to a traditional theological agenda fails to grapple with his decisive rejection of his role as a minister and as a believer. In the face of Schnapp's assertion that Baldwin never had "any argument with the gospel," the question is, of course, whether Baldwin's rejection of the white Christian god represents such an argument and how this rejection may go beyond his initial refusal of institutional expressions of Christianity. Even the most sophisticated interpretations that attempt simply to translate traditional notions of revelation into more modern secular notions like creativity

and insight do not register the extent to which Baldwin finds all forms of revelation burdensome, whether they be religious, secular, or profane. All forms of
revelation can be seen as fits of false consciousness and self-deception.[51] In
many ways, Baldwin's work begins to address the nature and reputed stability
of revelatory experience itself. Baldwin's rejection of Christianity goes beyond
simply criticizing the hypocritical character of institutional religion. His rejection, paired with how deeply connected he was to the burdens of his heritage,
grants a unique position from which to examine the very anatomy of a religious
tradition—a tradition that has been largely misunderstood and not critically
engaged. Baldwin in that speech before the WCC assured his audience that he
was not a theologian. Even so, he did not hesitate to suggest that the fact that he
had "left the pulpit" decades before gave him a special platform from which to
address them with authority. His credentials for addressing them consisted primarily of the rejection of his former ministry and their god.[52]

Sex, Hope, and Crisis in Black Holiness Culture

The credential of profound personal estrangement from a church he once
preached so fervently within granted Baldwin a perspective from which to see
the limitations and possibilities of a black holiness culture birthed in conflict
and tension. This mostly urban-centered religious movement had its beginnings
in the rural setting of the Mississippi Delta, where a group of black Baptists
revitalized and reconfigured the slave religion of their fathers and mothers for
a new century.[53] Baldwin intuitively understands this tense emerging reality of
an urban church culture and captures it for posterity in his first novel. In *Go
Tell It* we find a young John making his way in deeply contested territory
where the increasingly ephemeral rural past of his parents competes with a new
sensual urban reality filled with abundant opportunities to pursue very present
pleasures. Baldwin further dramatizes this tension with a coming-of-age narrative that reads as a spiritual rumination that implicitly criticizes the illusory
promise beneath religious piety and contests notions of salvation and community even as he embraces the vibrancy of religious theater. John Grimes on the
cusp of his manhood finds himself not only caught between the insular world
of his parents and gleaming city lights, but also in a struggle between the glory
and retribution promised by an ancient god and the urban possibilities created
by human beings who have the responsibility to save themselves. Baldwin, it
seems, faced all of these same tensions as he found a measure of hope and a
strong sense of crisis at the heart of black holiness culture.

    The title of this book, indeed, implies that Baldwin's work captures a sense
of how hope and crisis sit at the center of black evangelical expression in modern America. I will of course examine how Baldwin renders the theater of black

holiness culture in his plays, novels, and essays, but, more important, I hope to analyze how he deconstructs an often insular culture even as he employs its rhetoric for a broader cultural analysis of the United States that comes to animate his own political commitments. For Baldwin the erotic black body becomes the principal site from which we see this hope and crisis in black holiness culture. We can see this intermeshing of sex, promise, and alienation come together quite early in the course of Baldwin's fiction. An opening description of religious ecstasy in *Go Tell It* crackles with a bracing and brutally physical and sexual language. Early in the novel, Elisha, a musician on the brink of a fully realized manhood and friend to the young protagonist is overcome in the course of playing the piano for a late-night prayer meeting in a small sanctified church. In midchord, Elisha pushes himself away from the instrument and, looking up with "sightless eyes," dances and sways in a manner reminiscent of the spirit possession of his non-Christian ancestors. As Baldwin writes:

> He struck on the piano one last, wild note, and threw up his hands, palms upward, stretched wide apart. The tambourines raced to fill the vacuum left by his silent piano, and his cry drew answering cries. Then he was on his feet, turning, blind, his face congested, contorted with this rage, and the muscles leaping and swelling in his long, dark neck. It seemed that he could not breathe, that his body could not contain his passion, that he would be, before their eyes, dispersed into the waiting air. His hands, rigid to the very fingertips moved outward and back against his hips, his sightless eyes looked upward, and he began to dance. Then his hands closed into fists, and his head snapped downward, his sweat loosening the grease that slicked down his hair; and the rhythm of all the others quickened to match Elisha's rhythm; his thighs moved terribly against the cloth of his suit, his heels beat on the floor, and his fists moved beside his body as though he were beating his own drum. And so, for a while, in the center of the dancers, head down, fists beating, on, on, unbearably, until it seemed the walls of the church would fall for very sound; and then, in a moment, with a cry, head up, arms high in the air, sweat pouring from his forehead, and all his body dancing as though it would never stop. Sometimes he did not stop until he fell—until he dropped like some animal felled by a hammer—moaning, on his face. And then a great moaning filled the church.[54]

Baldwin's description of Elisha's "sightless eyes" hints at the limitations of this kind of encounter and the evangelical impulse it represents, while its strongly suggestive sexual imagery conjures life's dangerous energies, continued creativity, and possibilities. Although the rhetoric of the church conveys passion and life, it is also a language in crisis that since its beginnings has run up against the tragic limitations black people's exilic status imposes. Elisha's body represents this tension. It can barely contain the passion of his fierce religious dance to the percussive rhythms of the surrounding tambourines and of his own stomping feet as his sweaty body presses against his clothing. In that instant, Elisa's fluid form becomes the very embodiment of the conflict between the sacred and the profane that produced so much anxiety among black religious leaders at the turn of the twentieth century.

Baldwin's sensuous depiction of a single moment of religious ecstasy suggests that even as the conversion rituals of church holiness culture reveal the very flesh and blood of black life, they also reveal how tenuous the church's grip is on the potentially wayward sexual desires that it both fears and depends upon. Here instead, right after his description of an ecstatic Elisha, Baldwin reinforces this point with flashbacks to the pastor's earlier attempt to prevent Elisha and Ella Mae, a young woman and granddaughter of a prominent church member, from yielding to sexual temptation. During "a public warning" before the congregation, the pastor, Father James, accuses the couple of "walking disorderly" during a courtship barely discernable to outsiders. Father James of course notices the first signs of teenage lust and sees the "pitfalls Satan laid for the unwary" that he believes will lead inexorably to premarital sex. The minister works diligently to prevent any but the most minimal physical contact between Elisha and Ella Mae; he wants to ensure that any future coupling between the two will only come after they have made formal marital vows to one another.[55] Baldwin's description of the religious ecstasy of Elisha caught up in a holy dance is haunted with flashbacks of Father James that demonstrate the church's peculiar but deeply felt fear of sex. These paired passages show how church members are willing to condemn a sexual expressiveness that their own bodies in their dancing celebrate. This tension is at the heart of Baldwin's work.

Again and again, Baldwin, through his literary imagination in *Go Tell It* and his other novels, spills out fevered representations of ecstatic ebony bodies overwhelmed with a sexual passion they sometimes understand as divine. In the rest of my work here, I explore and situate this fundamental contradiction of church culture within the historical development of black evangelicalism in the United States and the complexities of Baldwin's own biography that has offered up these images of sexual bodies prancing before ancient gods. Elisha's black body reenacts the rituals of his displaced ancestors within a Christian universe. And even as his body pulses with life's rhythms, it represents a bridge for us from the ancient, pagan world to the new; it provides a platform for a contemporary interpretation of a strange, evangelical universe for today's world.

Chapter 2

Conversion, the Self, and Ugliness

black bodies before a white god

I was to hurt a great many people by being unable to imagine that anyone could possibly be in love with an ugly boy like me.

"INTRODUCTION: THE PRICE OF THE TICKET," *1985*

Although conversion and moments of religious ecstasy like that experienced by Elisha in *Go Tell It* are not the only markers that characterize the evangelical impulse in black religion, and American Protestantism more generally, they are significant ones. Their importance dates back to the colonial period with Puritans who began to emphasize a personal experience of rebirth and transformation. This emphasis helped to shape the development of a distinctive American Calvinism and influenced the later development of revivalism in the nineteenth century. Even so, many practitioners of Afro-Protestantism then as now did not experience the singular, traumatic event of conversion that Baldwin describes in his essays and fiction. After the Civil War, many black religious leaders established denominations independent from white people and developed a "social gospel" tradition of their own that would eventually culminate in the public career of Martin Luther King Jr. Leaders in this tradition typically chose to stress education, social progress, and racial uplift rather than to accent the importance of vivid conversion experiences, ring shouts, old spirituals, and various other aspects of slave religion and southern folk spirituality.[1]

Indeed, at the close of the nineteenth century, many religious and political elites within both the white and black communities eschewed the more openly emotive folk religiosity developed in the often multiracial camp meetings in the southern and western United States. For many whites the focus was on the need for social order in the wake of the Civil War, and for blacks the principal priority was to avoid lynching and other forms of state-sanctioned racial terror. This charged chaotic atmosphere helps to explain the mutual desire on the part of the majority of white and black religious and political elites to emphasize decorum and respectability. These leaders of both groups generally refused to embrace the folk religiosity and revivalism of the early cross-racial camp meetings that would eventually become the progenitors of the Pentecostal movement at the beginning of the twentieth century.[2]

Even so, the evangelical impulse still managed, especially in rural communities, to shape aspects of liturgical life in established black Baptist and Methodist churches. Even where a singular conversion experience was not emphasized, black religious communities still placed a high importance on the palpable immediacy of sacred presence and the acceptance of various forms of religious ecstasy that the metered singing, preaching, and rhythms of folk liturgical life often helped to engender. These aspects of black worship life demonstrate the extent of evangelicalism's sway on nearly all practitioners of Afro-Protestantism, whether or not they danced like Elisha in *Go Tell It* or embraced a "social gospel" ethic.[3] Despite these differences within black Protestantism, Baldwin, reflecting his own association with the holiness and Pentecostal movements within black religion, brought the initiation rite of conversion to the center of his critical and artistic reflections. His fixation with his own traumatic conversion is suggested in the long-standing working title—"Crying Holy"—of what would later become his first published novel, *Go Tell It*.

Paganlike Conversions: A Church in Labor

For Baldwin, intense conversion experiences not only characterized much of black religion but also were bridges where African or "pagan" sensibilities crossed over into Christianity. When Baldwin characterizes his own traumatic conversion in *Fire* it becomes the moment where he found "release" from guilt over his sexual desires in a "pagan" and "desperate" fashion.[4] In his last extended published essay, where he grapples with the Atlanta child murders, Baldwin again describes black religion in general as the blend of the pagan and the Christian. As he writes, "[W]hat the Blacks achieved [in Afro-Protestantism] and it cannot, now be undone, except by blowing up the universe . . . was to dig through the rubble, in Africa, in the Caribbean, and in North America, to find their ancestors, their gods, and themselves."[5] And indeed many Africans did see the intense conversions of evangelicalism as similar to various initiation rites their non-Christian ancestors performed. One enslaved woman in Virginia during the time of the Second Awakening reportedly shaved her head when she converted because "many of the slaves thought they could not be converted without doing this."[6] Such sentiments suggest that many Africans whose ancestors prepared their heads when mounted or possessed by African gods believed that in their Christian conversions they were mounted in like fashion by the Christian god. For these enslaved Africans, Christian conversion took place within a shared sacred domain where West African religious practices combined with those of evangelical Christianity.[7]

But whether conversion, from Baldwin's perspective, truly combines the pagan with the Christian, Baldwin certainly invokes the presence of his black Christian ancestors in his various descriptions of that traumatic encounter in Mount Calvary Pentecostal Faith Church found in his essays and most especially in his novel *Go Tell It*. What is clear is that communal expectations determine the significance and shape the meaning of the conversion event as much as the individual experience itself does, both for the new initiate and for the broader group of worshipers. In *Go Tell It*, the actual conversion of the protagonist, John Grimes, serves as the climax of the narrative and comprises almost the entire final section of the novel. The section entitled "Prayers of the Saints" precedes the climatic one entitled "The Threshing Floor" and consists of the individual stories of John's mother, stepfather, and aunt. John's conversion is nestled within the broader context of the spiritual and psychological striving and maturation of his immediate ancestors and guardians. "*His* [i.e., John's] choices are defined by things that have happened to other people, not him," Baldwin told one group of mostly black incarcerated women in the mid-1970s. "In short," Baldwin said, "he's walking into his ancestors' lives and experiences."[8] Echoing the Book of Hebrews, Baldwin tell us in *Go Tell It* that John's climatic conversion is performed before a "cloud of witnesses" and in the presence of John's relatives and ancestors, both known and unknown.[9]

Much of the anthropological work on black holiness culture mirrors Baldwin's depiction in *Go Tell It* in its description of conversion as a ritual of "becoming" and adulthood before an expectant religious community. One pair of anthropologists characterizes the typical holiness church as centered on "a ritual of potentiation" where various levels of contact with the Spirit are recognized through the collective religious practices of individual worshipers as they all attempt to "achieve oneness with the Spirit."[10] In *Go Tell It*, Baldwin describes John's conversion in very similar terms. For Baldwin, John's conversion represents a birthing into manhood that promises to loose him from the grip his father has on his current life and future destiny. Before John's conversion Baldwin anticipates this change in family dynamics that would ensue. As he writes,

John, who having lain in darkness, would no longer [after his conversion] be himself but some other man. He would have changed . . . he would have been born again. Then he would no longer be the son of his father, but the son of his Heavenly Father, the King. Then he need no longer fear his father, for he could take, as it were, their quarrel over his father's head to Heaven—to the Father who loved him, who had come down in the flesh to die for him. Then he and his father would be equals, in the sight, and the sound, and the love of God.[11]

With this conversion, John becomes his own person. The process enables John to establish an autonomous personality separate from his father's influence and control.

Baldwin anticipates this new birth into adulthood at the end of the second section with language suggestive of the rigors of childbirth. John is described as "the child" whose soul "struggled to light" on the threshing floor that becomes the stage where John will be overwhelmed by the power of God. Witnessing John's transformation on the threshing floor, the church, Baldwin describes, is "in labor" as they collectively call "on the name of Jesus," full of the pain that comes with birthing a new creation. So when the conversion, delayed until the final section, finally comes with all the tremors of childbirth and a kind of guttural intensity, we are not surprised. As Elizabeth, John's mother, muses about "that far-off day when John had come into the world," she hears John cry again, not with "the cry of a child" or "a newborn" but with the "bestial" howls of "the man-child" flung out while in the throes of religious ecstasy. When John finally falls "astonished beneath the power of the Lord," he falls not as child caught in the grasp of his father but as a man caught in the grasp of God.[12]

Fire, however, demonstrates that Baldwin's later reflections on his conversion experience did not radiate the hope and joy that birthing usually engenders. In this work, Baldwin portrays the conversion experience somewhat differently than he did in *Go Tell It*. Baldwin represents his own conversion, not only as a first step into adulthood but also as the beginning of a false consciousness that treasured heavenly visions and a sense of security over the ordinary dangers of life. As he writes, "I supposed Him to exist only within the walls of a church—in fact, of *our* church—and I supposed that God and safety were synonymous."[13] In this essay nearly a decade after his first novel was published, Baldwin described his religious encounter, what he calls a "religious crisis," as a safety valve from an outside world where unsympathetic white police authorities and pimps of all colors prey on young black men in Harlem. But more important, his conversion served as an escape from a newly unruly body overrun with sexual desire. Right before his conversion, ripe with an adolescent's self-doubt, he became "afraid" of an outside world filled with danger and what he called "the evil within me." Puberty and his deep fear of sex made his body a stranger to him. "I had no idea," Baldwin confesses in *Fire*, "what my voice, or my mind or my body was likely to do next." Religious and parental authorities accentuated this sense of alienation. Their notions of morality condemned his sexual desires (particularly for those of the same sex), and separated him from the pleasures of life. This alienation fostered a self-loathing that made him feel he was "one of the most depraved people on earth."[14]

In *Go Tell It* Baldwin hinted at these themes of alienation that would be in full flower in *Fire*. Even though Baldwin's exploration of the sexual dimension to this alienation is less explicit in *Go Tell It* than in his other works, the distinctive manner in which he links how Christian conversion to various expressions of estrangement—sexual and otherwise—is truly begun in this first novel. Teenage alienation is combined with an exploration of how notions of blackness converge with the issues of sexuality, shame, religion, and community in the young life of John Grimes. The very surname that John holds—Grimes—intimates that even as the eternal promises of the church express the vitality of a community, these same promises may in fact become bonds of imprisonment and remind readers how often blackness itself has been associated with grime, evil, death, and damnation. Indeed, for John in *Go Tell It* the promises of Christianity often seem more like the shackles of slavery than the delights of heaven. John chafes at a religion that keeps him from exploring the earthly pleasures he clearly hungers for. Baldwin establishes a traditional coming-of-age drama in the very first sentence: "Everyone had always said that John would be a preacher when he grew up, just like his father." But in the next breath, Baldwin reverses and subverts our expectations when he writes, "Not until the morning of his fourteenth birthday did he really begin to think about it and by then it was already too late."[15] With this last phrase—"by then it was already too late"—Baldwin suggests that the moment of reckoning may not be a welcome prospect for the young John. Perhaps John does not want to live out his life in the shadow of his father and his community's expectations.

Sex and Religious Ecstasy in Baldwin's Evangelical Culture

The development of religious ecstasy and the shout tradition in American evangelicalism is a history of the commingling of black and white worlds. The shout tradition according to some scholars emerged when the ecstatic conversion practices common among both Europeans and Africans combined with the largely African practice of religious dance.[16] For other scholars, despite evidence of ecstatic practices, the story of the shout tradition's emergence is primarily one of West African influence. From this perspective, African religious practices such as spirit possession fundamentally shaped the activities of all religious practitioners both black and white and actually "helped to fuel the

[Second] Awakening during its initial decades."[17] However the shout tradition of folk religious ecstasy actually developed, from early on, anxiety over racial commingling and the perennial worries that attend mixed groups of men and women in any context agitated religious leaders.

A general and widespread fear of sex combined insidiously with racial hostility to color the vision of various leaders and observers. These religious elites constantly worried about the links between erotic desire and the many bouts of religious enthusiasm that often occurred during camp meetings. Some critics obsessed over the dangers for "pristine" white women who, they feared, could be so caught up in religious fervor that they would unconsciously present their unprotected bodies before the "predatory" gazes of "virile" black men. They feared that their sisters and daughters might succumb to black men's reputed sexual prowess in the charged atmosphere of a revival. Describing the potential dangers for various cross-racial assignations, one "poetic" observer writes in 1810:

> She seem'd not to care
> Whether folks were disgusted or pleased
> Then a negro so strong,
> Full of faith and of song,
> View'd her charms thus expos'd to the weather
> He pity'd her case
> In the tone of free grace
> 'Till they lovingly walk'd off together.[18]

While the rumors of miscegenation ran rampant throughout the early decades of the nineteenth century, some questioned aloud whether the religious enthusiasm was "more wanton amours than religious zeal."[19] Given this complicated and tense history over sex, Baldwin's examination of the relationship between religious ecstasy and sexual expression is truly provocative. With his description in *Go Tell It* of Gabriel as a self-righteous hypocrite, Baldwin takes a critical stance not unlike rationalists during the Great Awakening who questioned whether ecstatic religious conversions provided the firm foundation necessary for the consistent moral life that reason did. In the course of his early work, Baldwin begins to reckon with the long legacy of sexual tension that often hid beneath the stated suspicions of those who suspected illicit sexual activity between men and women—blacks and whites—during the camp meetings of American revivalism since the early nineteenth century.

Baldwin suggests a kinship between religious pursuits and sexual play throughout his work. In *Go Tell It*, this connection between religious and sexual feeling is clearly drawn in the observations of the hated stepfather, Gabriel, who compares the music of the nightclubs with that of storefront churches. For Gabriel, the music echoing from the clubs is not "the music of the saints but another music, infernal which glorified lust and held righteousness up to scorn." Through the party haze, the misogynist Gabriel looks at the women there with disgust. He thinks they should stay at home and teach "their grandchildren how to pray." But instead, Gabriel finds them "night after night, twisting their bodies into lewd hallelujahs in smoke-filled, gin-heavy dance halls, singing to their loving man."[20] Even writing from this self-righteous stance Baldwin manages to describe the juke joints of southern Louisiana nightlife as places where the sacred and profane meet and move together in the gyrations of women who have a love for "sin" and for the movement of their sensuous bodies. Although Gabriel sees a sharp distinction between the two worlds, it is clear that Baldwin himself sees lust and desire beneath it all. The women might have offered only "lewd hallelujahs," but they were expressions of praise all the same.

Baldwin goes beyond simply suggesting these connections between sexual and religious feeling; he also offers a criticism of conversion-brokered religious perspectives that considers the often-transient character of these same conversion experiences where the sincere desire for holiness can give way suddenly to a most rancid hypocrisy. Baldwin pursues this criticism indirectly in an essay published in 1985, where he discusses whether large groups of people are capable of achieving collective atonement. In this essay, Baldwin suggests that while intense conversions may air out repressed emotions of fear and self-loathing, they do not fundamentally change lives for the better. In describing the often "transitory" character of conversion he shows how "the reformed" drunk and others addicted to self-destructive behaviors often return "to their former ways."[21] In fact, in Baldwin's view, the effects of intense conversions can be worse than a meaningless form of emotional release; it may, in fact, foster a dangerous self-righteousness.

In his description of Gabriel, the stepfather of the young John Grimes, Baldwin offers a damning portrayal of religious hypocrisy and overweening self-righteousness. Gabriel's story dramatically demonstrates how conversion-based religion can have all the ethical stability of a one-night stand. Even though Gabriel's conversion initially does appear to shape his consciousness, his passions and commitment for the holy dissipate as quickly as they were once so intensely felt. In Baldwin's story, Gabriel is converted shortly after a night of sex. Flush with how he and an older woman had just "rocked in their bed of sin," Gabriel is suddenly caught short when the birds and other animals fall quiet, seemingly hushed by a silence strangely charged with the judgment of God. "[A]ll creation had been stilled," Baldwin writes, "before the just and awful wrath of God." As Gabriel touches a nearby tree to hide from God's anger, he cries for mercy and achieves in this moment "a new beginning, a blood-washed day" that leads to a new life as a married man and a Baptist minister.[22] But this "blood-washed day" does not ultimately prevent Gabriel from having an affair several years later and then treating his mistress and the child they conceived together as "an expendable moral lesson," as Baldwin scholar Trudier Harris quite rightly describes it. When his mistress, Esther, tells Gabriel of her pregnancy, he forsakes any sense of responsibility and leaves her to travel alone to Chicago with money he steals from his wife, Deborah. As Harris explains,

> Gabriel has done an excellent job of convincing himself that he is good and pure and that he has escaped the life that found him drunk and vomit-covered so many mornings. It would shatter his image of himself beyond reclamation if he were to admit that he is at fault in the affair with Esther. He must therefore tell himself that he is the superior being who is being tested, who is being tempted by the luscious fare served before him. He is like Jesus in the wilderness confronted by the Devil, and it is a test of his will that he must overcome Esther's temptations. His participation in the affair pales, then, in comparison with the superhuman strength with which he extricates himself from his fallen status.[23]

The ultimate result of Gabriel's self-righteous self-delusion is death for both Esther, who dies alone shortly after childbirth, and for their son, who dies still unrecognized by his biological father more than fifteen years later. Gabriel's selfishness is foreshadowed from the very beginning with his initial conversion. Before his moment of redemption, it is clear that Gabriel sees his coming conversion not as an opportunity for humble repentance, but rather as a chance to grasp power for his own ends. "[H]e desired in his soul," Baldwin writes, "all the glories that his mother prayed he should find." Gabriel wants to have power, "to be master," and to speak with divine authority.[24] Given his power-hungry, selfish ways, we are not surprised to hear Gabriel respond to Esther's disclosure with an abrupt "I got God's work to do—my life don't belong to you. Nor to that baby, neither."[25] Despite Gabriel's conversion-brokered religion, Esther and their child, it seems, fall outside the scope of his moral vision.

The story of Gabriel was the beginning of a pattern in Baldwin's fiction where traditional religious faith bred dangerous emotional callousness. This development reached its apotheosis in Baldwin's *If Beale Street Could Talk* in the mid-1970s. There, in his portrayal of the pious Alice Hunt, the mother of Tish's beau, Baldwin explicitly links Hunt's callousness with her propensity for the joys of religious ecstasy and characterizes her as a lazy hypocrite. At the start of the novel, the protagonist, Tish, describes Hunt as "that woman [who] fell out happy in church without knowing the whereabouts of her only son." In the words of Alice's husband, Frank: "Whatever Alice don't feel like being bothered with . . . she leaves in the hands of the Lord."[26] So for Baldwin, religion was not simply insular; it also prompted its adherents to shirk the basic responsibilities of life. Religion became for Baldwin the central promoter of emotional deadness and even parental irresponsibility. Gabriel in *Go Tell It*, Margaret in *The Amen Corner*, and Alice in *Beale Street* all allow their religious aspirations to threaten basic familial connections between parents and children. Leaving aside for now the gender bias in his portrayal of religious women, what is remarkable about Baldwin's depiction of Gabriel as a lapsed minister goes beyond his implicit criticism of conversion-brokered religion. Baldwin uses this very analysis of religion and translates it into what will become his analysis of whiteness as a social identity. If whiteness is based on self-delusion, then, as Baldwin seems to suggest, those trapped in it can only bring the same level of death that Gabriel's actions did. The social identity of whiteness has all the earmarks of misguided religious devotion. Or perhaps it brings all the callousness and deadness of spirit, as one Baldwin critic describes it, that comes from having "no self-consciousness" of one's own "apostasy."[27]

The Black Body and the Ugliness of Self-Loathing

Even as Gabriel's story highlights the challenges of conversion-brokered religion, Baldwin also explores the nature of conversion itself. From the beginning of *Go Tell It*, Baldwin represents the conversion of John both as a communal celebration of adulthood and individual transformation, and as an expression of social control from a rigid, religious community. The expressed need for social control, though predicated on a desire for safety from an unjust, dangerous world, becomes the mechanism through which a great familial curse is handed down to untold generations of black people. In *Fire* Baldwin addresses more explicitly than he does in *Go Tell It* what he sees as the relationship between self-hate and black Christian identity. In beginning to explain black self-loathing, Baldwin references the so-called Hamitic curse from Genesis, which slaveholders used to legitimatize the naturalness of their enslavement of African peoples.[28] Writing from the perspective of black people, Baldwin explains, "In the same way that we, for white people, were the descendants of Ham, and were cursed forever, white people were, for us, the descendants of Cain. And the passion with which we loved the Lord was a measure of how deeply we feared and distrusted and, in the end, hated almost all strangers, always, and avoided and despised ourselves."[29] Baldwin is willing to confront how black people have "avoided and despised" themselves, and he is determined to link Christian conversion not only with the celebratory impulses of any communal initiation but also with those religious sensibilities that foster self-loathing by restricting healthy sexual expression.

An early folktale, labeled by its unsympathetic recorder as an "uncouth legend," highlights aspects of the self-hatred many see as a backdrop to the emergence of black Christian commitment. In the legend the black body itself is depicted as the creation of the devil done against the "commands of God." The story begins with the devil "flung into hell" as punishment for acting against God's will. The devil is then "tied" to "de wheel er de chariot er fire!" And there, the devil, as the story continues, was "[c]hained ter de turnin' wheel er fire; en dar he gwine stay twel de great Risin' Day. The devil succeeding only in forming the shape of a man and without the soul, became as it were, a creator of death, but there come no life, dar come no breaf! But de Lo'd he feel's sorry for the dead man dat he gin him breaf en er soul same as er white man."[30] Some quite persuasively see this story as a commentary on the equality of all human beings and the depths of divine mercy. Many also point to the devil's failure to create a person with a soul as a description of the demonic underpinnings of a slavery system that tries to usurp the creative powers of God even as it creates dead husks of humanity stripped of divine substance. As Riggins Earl writes, "The [enslaved Africans] understood their own creation as the result of the mercy of God. Despite all the attempts of the satanic forces of slavery to make them into that which was less than human, only God was recognized as having the power to make the black body sacred."[31] Even so, the story's worldview adopts white supremacist notions that associate black skin with wickedness and the devil. While those storytellers clearly do not accept Western culture's tendency to see black people as embodied evil, there is certainly a widespread tendency among some black people to adopt the color symbolism of their enslavers. Echoing an old hymn that still reverberates in black churches across the country, Baldwin describes in an early essay how some black people boisterously sing, "Wash me . . . and I shall be whiter, whiter than snow!" And as they sing this petition to a white god, they implicitly acknowledge how much separates them from their adopted deity. The hymn's words suggest a gulf that cannot be bridged without the sacrifice of black people's sense of worthiness. They were made by a divine creator, indeed, "but not," as Baldwin opines, "in His image."[32]

Under the weight of this dubious heritage, we are not surprised to hear Baldwin describe his father's bearing and appearance with just a hint of condescension. In his famous essay "Notes of a Native Son," Baldwin describes his father as looking like pictures he had seen of "African Tribal chieftains" with "war-paint on barbaric mementos, standing among spears." For Baldwin, his father was beautiful in his deep blackness, but to his father's misfortune he "did not know that he was beautiful."[33] Even as he condemns his father's lack of vision, Baldwin also betrays how hard it is for many to see the beauty in blackness. Baldwin's own capacity for the black self-hatred he accuses his father of is also displayed here. In the early 1950s, it seems that even Baldwin, much like his white liberal interlocutors, before he had even set foot on African land, closely associated blackness with barbarism and an animalistic warlike primitivism.

But Baldwin's own hidden assumptions only reflect to a small degree those of the larger culture where there were widely shared assumptions of black inferiority. These notions took root even before the founding of the republic. Europeans had long associated blackness with sin and sensuality. So when various British travelers encountered the "heathenism" of black people they quickly linked their dark skin to these same attributes.[34] For these direct ancestors of the American colonists, black people were cast beyond the moral universe of Christianity. They became not simply strangers and aliens unfamiliar with Western ways but black devils who cavorted with minions from the underworld. The term *devil* "mediates" — as Winthrop Jordan explains in his influential historical study on American attitudes toward black people — both the "barbarity" and "heathenism" inherent in English notions of blackness and represents black people as actual embodiments of evil. "[N]egroes bear on their foreheads the marks of the reprobation," one missionary of the colonial period writes.[35]

But despite these connections that Baldwin himself does not entirely avoid, when John Grimes, like the author that created him, suffers for his unusual looks, it still comes with a troubling jolt for the contemporary reader. In an early scene where John receives his weekend cleaning assignments from his mother instead of the birthday gift he had been hoping for, the young man looks up from his morning labors and fully expects to see Satan in the reflecting glass where his face should be. Baldwin writes:

> [H]e took from the small bucket under the sink the dustrag . . . and returned to the living-room to excavate, as it were, his family's goods and gear. Thinking bitterly of his birthday, he attacked the mirror with the cloth, watching his face appear as out of a cloud. With a shock he saw that his face had not changed, that the hand of Satan was as yet visible. His father had always said that his face was the face of Satan — and was there not something — in the lift of the eyebrow, in the way his rough hair formed a V on his brow — that bore witness to his father's words?[36]

At the end of *Go Tell It*, references to the so-called Hamitic curse frame John's climatic conversion even as this cleaning scene filled with his self-doubt frames the entire novel. These concerns about his physical appearance simply demonstrate how deeply held John's self-loathing truly is. The shame that society's condemnation of same-sex desire foists on the young John is skillfully coupled throughout *Go Tell It* with the traditional coming-of-age themes—forever keeping the potential for transformation tied to that of self-loathing and sexual repression. At the moment of John's greatest vulnerability, Baldwin ends the story just as he began. John, perched on the brink of adulthood alone without the prospect of "human or heavenly help," hears an "ironic voice" that scornfully inquires whether he believes that he and all black people are "cursed" and bear the stain of Ham.[37] John's conversion establishes him as a man in the presence of a community of persons both alive and dead. But this same conversion acts as a vehicle of social control where a community's distrust of sex can be actualized in the intensification of John's personal self-loathing.

John is never far from "the narrow and dirty" room he finds himself cleaning at the beginning of the novel. It is here in this room that John sees his face as that of Satan, fully accepting the lie his father told him, just as a young Jimmy Baldwin accepted what his father told him. In *The Devil Finds Work* Baldwin describes how his father called him "the ugliest boy he had ever seen." And while Baldwin claims his father's verdict was "more resounding than real," he acknowledges that this judgment had a "decidedly terrifying effect" on his later life.[38] Baldwin's father saw real societal limits for any young black boy no matter how precocious he might be. When asked whether his father affected his sense of what he could do in the world, Baldwin answered, "My father did one thing for me. He said, 'You can't do it.'" And when the interviewer pushed Baldwin to elaborate on why precisely his father thought he could not succeed, Baldwin answered: "Because I was black, because I was little, because I was ugly. He made me ugly."[39]

And it is this ugliness that later disrupts Baldwin's ability to accept love. Ugliness does not simply describe a lack of attractiveness; in the context of Baldwin's life, ugliness is linked with a blackness that circumscribes and restricts the life chances of those who labor within its concealment and are unable to give or accept love. As Baldwin confesses in a later essay, "I was to hurt a great many people by being unable to imagine that anyone could possibly be in love with an ugly boy like me."[40] For Baldwin, the god of Christianity became a kind of "primal father" who sees black people as ugly; this disregard sets the context for why so many black people find ways not to love themselves or each other.[41] And Baldwin's sense of his own ugliness, while extreme, fully intersected with his sense of the much broader societal realities of black shame. In an interview with Studs Terkel in 1961, Baldwin labeled this shame as "one of the great psychological hazards of being an American Negro." As Baldwin told Terkel, "Every Negro in America is in one way or another menaced by it [shame]. One is born in a white country . . . [and] when you open your eyes on the world, everything you see: none of it applies to you." For Baldwin, Christianity and its white god fully contributed to this culture of shame. As Baldwin again confessed to Terkel: "All this got terribly mixed together in my mind with the Holy Roller, White God business. I really began to go a little out of my mind. Obviously I wasn't white . . . but I didn't quite know anymore what being *black* meant."[42]

In his controversial play, *Blues for Mister Charlie*, produced in the mid-1960s, Baldwin connects his inner turmoil over whiteness to a broader understanding of how the self-hate endemic to the Christianity of his ancestors shaped and limited contemporary black experience. In the play, a disillusioned minister, Meridian, tries to cope both with his son's murder and with the strong possibility that his son's killer—a white racist and established shopkeeper in town—may avoid any community or legal sanctions. In speaking to a local white liberal reporter, Meridian muses about his identity as a Christian and whether his religion gives him any real capacity to fight back and maintain a semblance of dignity in the face of white terrorism. Meridian says:

> I'm a Christian. I've been a Christian all my life, like my Mama and Daddy before me and like their Mama and Daddy before them. Of course, if you go back far enough, you get to a point *before* Christ, if you see what I mean, B.C.—and at that point, I've been thinking black people weren't raised to turn the other cheek, and in the hope of heaven. No, then they didn't have to take low. Before Christ. They walked around just as good as anybody else, and when they died, they didn't go to heaven, they went to join their ancestors.[43]

Even though he is a Christian preacher, Meridian wonders aloud whether the gospel that he preaches has been a blessing or a curse. For his son, it is clearly a curse because if Christian legends are to be believed, Meridian knows that his murdered son now resides in hell. Relying on his sense of West African traditions, Meridian believes that if black people had never come in contact with Christianity, his son would be forever in the company of his ancestors. Meridian's parental devotion forces him to wonder whether this is really "such a mighty advance" for his son to be consigned to hell.[44] Richard would have been better off, Meridian concludes, in a world where Christian symbols did not so fundamentally shape the meaning of black lives both before and after death.

But Meridian's concern extends beyond just his own son to embrace black people as a whole. Throughout his speech with Parnell, Meridian is conflicted about the merits of the church he represents, and he wonders whether Christianity has actually been a curse not just for his son but also for black people generally. Even so, as he speculates about what was previously unthinkable, he paradoxically begins to believe that the only chance his ancestors had for dignity in bondage was from within this Christian curse. At one point Meridian says: "Maybe I *had* to become a Christian in order to have any dignity at all. Since I wasn't a man in men's eyes, then I could be a man in the eyes of God."[45] Indeed, observers of Afro-Protestant worshipers have long argued that a principal reason for enslaved Africans' appropriation of evangelical Christianity was the direct access to divine acceptance that evangelical conversion experiences promised. Their unworldly origins could provide black people a platform beyond the human machinations of their enslavers from which to stand against the terror their white oppressors might impose.[46]

But despite the dignity conversion to Christianity conferred, Baldwin saw the church as cursed because of its condemnation of black bodies and Christians' desire for security in the next life over their embrace of this one. These sentiments contributed to the developing sense among many black people that they could not trust their own experience. But before their encounter with the Christian gospel African people, as Meridian says, "walked around just as good as anybody else." Given the legacy of bondage, their heirs in North America could not help but consider themselves less worthy than their white counterparts. Even so, Baldwin believed that the organized black churches, no matter how compromised, were the last terrain from which a beleaguered people, stripped of their connections to their African homeland, could forge a new identity and achieve some measure of collective social power. In an interview published initially during the late 1970s, Baldwin seemed to accept the words of Kalamu ya Salaam, his interviewer, that "the church has not proven to have been the redemptive force" black people have needed. But Baldwin was also quick to add that the "church was how we [black people] forged our identity."[47] With the connections to African gods severed, the bible and the church were nearly all American blacks had to fashion an identity that could withstand the hardships white supremacy imposes. And even though Christianity's symbolic world seemed to equate the black with the ugly and the damned, the church was the principal institutional structure that housed the biblical symbols and the acts of worship that would provide one of the few platforms for resistance. The fact that this institution was so compromised from its very inception captures how a sense of the tragic defines black life in the United States.

The links Baldwin clearly draws between Christianity and black self-loathing in *Blues* are not as fully realized in *Go Tell It*. Even so, Baldwin in his first novel does engage, even if less explicitly, how black self-loathing and Christianity are interwoven in black life. Although John emerges a more fully realized adult person, Baldwin, with his descriptions of John's constricted reality, suggests that his future life possibilities may not be as boundless as readers would hope. A precocious John can only hope that he does not experience his moment of conversion and manhood as the total imposition of the community's will and his father's will on his own. John's deep reluctance to embrace the faith of his parents ultimately springs from a deep love of learning and his fear and hatred of his father. As Baldwin writes:

> John cherished something that his father could not reach. It was his hatred and his intelligence that he cherished, the one feeding the other. He lived for the day when his father would be dying and he, John, would curse him on his deathbed. And this was why, though he had been born in the faith and had been surrounded all his life by the saints and by their prayers and their rejoicing, and though the tabernacle in which they worshipped was more completely real to him than the several precarious homes in which he and his family had lived, John's heart was hardened against the Lord.[48]

So, given this initial reluctance, it is not surprising that even at the height of his encounter with the divine at the novel's climax, John still hears an "ironic" voice urging him to get up from the threshing floor "if he did not want to become like all the other niggers."[49]

John's black body and its reputed ugliness limit the reach of his ambitions. Throughout *Go Tell It*, when black bodies are described they are invariably labeled as ugly or sinful. The most striking example of how Baldwin links blackness to ugliness comes during a flashback in the novel's final climatic section when John remembers an incident just as his conversion begins. In the flashback, John walks with his father, Gabriel, and sees an elderly woman whose appearance reminds him of his mother and himself.

> Then, coming up this straight and silent street, he saw a woman, very old and black coming toward them, staggering on the crooked stones. She was drunk and dirty, and very old, and her mouth was bigger than his mother's mouth, or his own; her mouth was loose and wet, and he had *never* seen anyone so black. His father was astonished to see her, and beside himself with anger; but John was glad. He clapped his hands and cried: "See! She's uglier than Mama! She's uglier than me!" "You mighty proud, ain't you," his father said, "to be the Devil's son?"[50]

Perhaps Gabriel gives this angry response because he believes the woman is a prostitute and this only reminds him anew of John's bastard status. Whatever the case may be, the description of the woman emphasizes her thick African lips and depicts her as uniquely black in color. Beyond any intimations of prostitution, it is her features clearly stamped with the imprint of Africa that prompt the young John to cry of her ugliness; he ties the unsightly together with the black and the African.

To be ugly in Baldwin's world is to be without love—in isolation from others; it is to live a life where there is only self-hate. In this world, ugliness becomes the physical manifestation of self-loathing. It represents the unattractiveness of a shame that distorts people's perceptions of themselves as they relate to the outside world. In an essay published in the late 1950s, Baldwin touches on these interlocking issues when he describes his long exile from the United States and how it shaped his psychology. Baldwin confesses: "I was as isolated from Negroes as I was from whites which is what happens when a Negro at bottom believes what white people say about him."[51] Baldwin's attempt to escape shame and his ultimate refusal to believe what white people said about him is what finally propelled him away from the church and away from the country of his birth.

In *Go Tell It*, Baldwin dramatizes most acutely how impoverished circumstances and Christian teaching foster self-loathing in the early story of John Grimes. The scene in the book that best illustrates the interwoven character of Christianity, shame, and the constricted life of poverty for black people is where the young John "with shame and horror" cleans the grimy, narrow room his mother assigns him and confronts his own feelings of bitterness and defilement. In this room dirt "triumphed beneath the sink" and "roaches spawned" no matter how hard John cleaned. This grimy room symbolically tied so firmly to the limitations and restrictions of black life is of course almost-mockingly decorated with Christian plaques of Scripture verses that celebrate the possibility of salvation. As John cleans the grimy, narrow room he curses with an "angry hardness of heart" beneath his breath at his Sisyphean task: *"He who is filthy, let him be filthy still."*[52] As long as John stays within this reality his religion seems to endorse, his body is condemned as ugly and his sexual desires damned as sinful; no effort he exerts while trapped in this narrow existence will ultimately allow him to experience all life has to offer. No mater how triumphant his conversion seems, if he stays within the limited scope of his church there is only futility. This pronouncement early in the novel makes the closing acts all the more ominous. In that final section when John finally has his encounter with the Almighty, Baldwin begins with a biblical passage from Isaiah where the prophet woefully proclaims that he is "a man of unclean lips" from "a people of unclean lips."[53] Even before John's experience of wonder begins, the reader, in fact, wonders, given this apparent impossibility of cleansing, whether there is any hope for John and black people as a whole if they are seen as a people with unclean lips and defiled hearts.

The only hope for John, in fact, is to escape his parents' world and to follow the intellectual promise he first demonstrates in school as he struggles to separate from the shackles of his comforting religious birthright. When the young John at the opening of the novel receives praise from his principal as "a very bright boy," like a young Jimmy Baldwin had in P.S. 24, this encouragement becomes a "shield" from outside troubles. But unlike the promises of religion that lay claim to possibilities of eternity, Baldwin notes that this shield does not promote insularity and dependence on a divine savior to rescue broken human beings. Human beings have the capacity within themselves to rescue each other. We see this as Baldwin writes about John, clearly remembering how good he felt when he himself received praise from Gertrude Ayer, the first black principal of New York City.[54] John, Baldwin writes, understands in that moment that he had "a power"—his mind—that others lacked to "save himself, to raise himself."[55] Outside the confines of religion, Baldwin sees the possibility of a labor that is fruitful and not wasted in the hopes of illusionary sacred delights. In *The Amen Corner* Baldwin, as mentioned in chapter 1, is even more explicit in his depiction of the life-denying restrictions religion can bring. Luke, David's father and Margaret's estranged husband, tells his wife a hard truth. Even though he knows that she is worried about how their son is pressing to leave the church and his mother's embrace, Luke tells her: "I don't care what kind of life he lives—as long as it's *his* life—not mine, not his mama's, but his own. I ain't going to let you make him safe."[56] Luke seems to speak the words that Baldwin wished his own father had uttered as he left home to find his own life without the comforts of church or country.

Christianity as Slavery: The Shame and Displacement of Christian Conversion

Since the very beginning of his published work, Baldwin went beyond these characterizations of conversion we have already discussed and equates Christianity with American chattel slavery itself. In his early essay "Everybody's Protest Novel," which first brought him to the attention of the literary circles in New York, Baldwin links "protest novels" like Harriet Beecher Stowe's *Uncle Tom's Cabin* to the West's missionary efforts in Africa. As Baldwin writes, "[T]he aim of the protest novel becomes something very closely resembling the zeal of those alabaster missionaries to Africa to cover the nakedness of the natives, to hurry them into the pallid arms of Jesus and thence into slavery."[57] With this historical understanding, Baldwin sees Christian conversion not simply as an initiation rite into a new faith, but as an emblem of displacement for those Africans snatched from their homeland and forced into a "New World." For these displaced Africans and perhaps for many of their progeny, the principal backdrop of Christian conversion is shame, not hope.

In his essay "Many Thousands Gone," written in the early 1950s, Baldwin reminds his readers that unlike other American citizens, "the past was taken" from black people. They did not voluntarily reject past ties in their "adoption" of a new homeland. Appreciating this history burdened with loss, Baldwin grapples with how the involuntary presence of black people carries a shame inscribed in the very countenance and bodies of these displaced children of Africa. Writing from the perspective of the white majority, Baldwin considers the meaning of this shame both for blacks and whites:

> [H]is [i.e., black people's] shameful history was carried, quite literally, on his brow. Shameful; for he was heathen as well as black and would never have discovered the healing blood of Christ had not we braved the jungles to bring him these glad tidings. Shameful; for, since our role as missionary had not been wholly disinterested, it was necessary to recall the shame from which we had delivered him in order more easily to escape our own. As he accepted the alabaster Christ and the bloody cross, . . . he must henceforth, accept that image we then give him of himself: having no other and standing, moreover, in danger of death should he fail to accept the dazzling light thus brought into such darkness. It is this quite simple dilemma that must be borne in mind if we wish to comprehend his psychology.[58]

In his first novel the possible connections of self-loathing and conversion are suggested, but here, before his novel is even published, Baldwin demonstrates just how closely aligned he believes the psychology of black self-hatred to be with the very act of Christian conversion itself. As he considers his own capacity for self-hatred, Baldwin confronts the blackness and the pre-Christian status of African "heathens" of long ago. In so doing, he exposes the broad reach of white supremacy and the shame of white Americans' avoidance of history and their complicity with the death-giving legacy of an "alabaster Christ," a "bloody cross," and an angry imperialism.

Because they remind Westerners with their very presence of this bloody legacy of conquest, black people become in Baldwin's view the great outcasts and intruders in Western culture. Considering this keen sense of alienation, Baldwin sees his exilic life and his wounded psyche as a metaphor for the black experience in the United States. Baldwin himself feels this alienation most keenly before the wonders of Western art, architecture, and civilization. In the autobiographical notes for *Notes of a Native Son* he confesses that before the cathedral at Chartres and other products of medieval European culture he was "an interloper." But Baldwin's response to the artifacts of Western culture says as much about his relationship to what it means to be black as it does about his relationship with Western culture. He confesses that although he "hated and feared white people," it did not mean that he "loved black people." Actually Baldwin writes: "I despised them, possibly because they failed to produce Rembrandt."[59]

Central to this black shame, Baldwin believes, is the distortion in black self-image intrinsic to the black worship of a white god. Describing the compromised position of black people on their arrival to the "New World," Baldwin writes: "Thus, the African exile, pagan hurried off the auction block and into the fields fell on his knees before that God in Whom he must now believe; Who had made him, but not in His image." This distorted black self-image overflows into the hymns sung and the iconography embraced. So while the religion most black people accept holds the promise that divine "vengeance will be exacted" on their white oppressors, this same promise is undercut when the exiled African sings, "Wash me and I shall be whiter, whiter than snow."[60] The promise of divine judgment is further undermined when the black Christian fails to recognize how black people and the devil—the very personification of evil—are presumed to be close kin because they share the same color in Western Christianity's symbolic universe.

This focus on the intimacies of worship demonstrates how Baldwin takes the tension between African and American identities that W. E. B. Du Bois famously describes in *The Souls of Black Folk* and translates it into the personal psychological space where there is love and hate—desire and fear. Where Du Bois writes about a feeling of "twoness" and the clash of "two warring ideals" in "one dark body" held together by sheer determination, Baldwin refuses to see the possibilities of reconciliation and "self-conscious manhood" that Du Bois hopes for. Du Bois assures his mostly white audience that black people would not, in fact, "Africanize America" and promises that these exiled children of Africa only want the opportunity to be both black and American without "being cursed and spit upon."[61] But even as his own work resonates with the most important and influential black intellectual of the twentieth century, Baldwin sees little room for the optimism found in the early work of Du Bois.[62] Baldwin sees instead a "catalogue of brutality" that has bred a reality and "nightmare notion" of black self-hate expressed in the desire to be white. A reality, Baldwin writes, that a black person "both flees and rushes to embrace."[63] Instead of the two warring ideals, Baldwin describes the condition of black people in America with the language of addiction. He sees a disquieted, disfigured black people addicted to the very notion of whiteness. In Baldwin's world, black people seem forever tied to a desire for things white and the status they bring; they love it even as they hate that they love it. "You become a collaborator, an accomplice of your own murderers," Baldwin tells poet Nikki Giovanni in one televised conversation, "because you believe the same things they do." And what white people seem to believe most, in Baldwin's estimation at least, is their own superior status as compared to that of shameful blacks. And black people seem to believe the same and more. Baldwin then goes on to explain the basic psychology that structures contemporary racial identity: "They [white people] think it's important to be white and you [black people] think it's important to be white; they think it's a shame to be black and you think it's a shame to be black."[64]

When Baldwin attempts to escape this dilemma of black self-hatred, circumstances force him to see anew the possibility of divine disregard and even malevolence as he considers the apparent permanence of black suffering. This terrible vision of God links him with his older fellow traveler, Du Bois, who rages at God after scores of black people are killed over some days during race riots in Atlanta in 1906. Marveling at how police confiscated the guns of black Atlantans even as they allowed white people in the area to remain armed and maraud through the streets, killing and beating black people in local parks and stores, Du Bois raises the specter of a silent, passive god. This god appears to turn a blind eye to an increasing "flood of innocent blood." Du Bois pleads against this divine silence as he prays: "Sit not longer blind, Lord God, deaf to our prayers and dumb to our dumb suffering. Surely Thou, too art not white, O Lord, a pale bloodless heartless thing!"[65] Here, Du Bois in the midst of his desperate plea is a critique of white identity as he links the social identity of whiteness to lifelessness.

As he often does, Baldwin casts God's apparent passivity in even more personal terms. Baldwin wants to have a fistfight with the god white America worships. In the voice of a protagonist in one of his later novels, Baldwin dismantles the notion of manifest destiny that animates the sense of many in the United States who see their nation as a special instrument of the divine will. Baldwin issues this challenge to God and God's servants: "I don't think America is God's gift to anybody—if it is, God's days have *got* to be numbered. That God these people say they serve—and do serve . . . has got a nasty sense of humor. Like you'd beat the shit out of Him, if He was a man. Or: if *you* were."[66] The widespread acceptance of this god by both blacks and whites becomes for Baldwin a threat to his very manhood. Divine silence is not just frustratingly mysterious, as Du Bois suggests, but in the face of such clear continued inequality the silence appears malevolent. While Du Bois fears that this Christian god may be white, Baldwin knows that he is.

Chapter 3

"Just as Black"

a malevolent god and the
permanence of black suffering

And the blood of the Lamb had not cleansed me in any way whatever. I was just as black as I had been the day that I was born.

<small>THE FIRE NEXT TIME, *1963*</small>

S hortly after the murder of Martin Luther King Jr., Baldwin found himself taking King's place at the podium in Uppsala, Sweden, before the World Council of Churches in 1968. Before the tragic events in Memphis, where the civil rights leader and Nobel laureate was cut down during the course of his support for the city's striking and mostly black sanitation workers, the international church organization had already scheduled King as a principal speaker for the occasion. At that borrowed podium, Baldwin remembered how the life of another fallen Baptist minister, his father, David Baldwin, also ended tragically. James told the gathered audience that his father had given "his life to the Christian faith" with "stunning and painful results."[1] Sometime later, in *No Name in the Street*, Baldwin describes what in fact these "stunning and painful results" were, echoing earlier descriptions of his father's crippling paranoia and insanity that bedeviled and gripped his mind and forced him into a mental health facility during his last years. Given "his *unreciprocated* love" for God, his son speculates that "it is no wonder our father went mad."[2]

The sense of divine disregard that appears in Baldwin's 1968 speech is prefigured in *Go Tell It*, published fifteen years earlier. Gabriel Grimes, David Baldwin's literary alter ego, burdened with his abandonment of his mistress, Esther, and their unborn son, tries to distract himself from the weight of his own heavy conscience. To escape self-condemnation and evade personal responsibility, Gabriel muses about the dismal state of black people and how this oppressed people in the course of their migration to the North had in fact "wandered from God." His musings only demonstrate how quickly Gabriel's sense of moral responsibility can be eclipsed as he focuses on the role white elites played in the exilic aimlessness and suffering of black people rather than on his own culpability. Even as he pushes aside his own guilt, Gabriel sees evidence of gross injustice everywhere and hears the cries for vengeance from the spilled blood of black people caught beneath the thumb of white oppression. "There seemed no door, anywhere," Baldwin's Gabriel says, where "blood did not call out, unceasingly, for blood." Grappling with this indictment even as he evades the tawdriness of his own narcissistic exploits, Gabriel blames those white men for prostituting black women and humiliating black men.[3]

In the midst of his own keen desire for any relief from his deserved guilt, Gabriel finds a Christian god who promises divine judgment and retribution against white exploiters even while remaining largely hidden and aloof before the widespread black suffering Gabriel so vividly recounts. In fact, from Gabriel's perspective this god seems to purposefully turn away from his entreaties for personal restoration and communal redemption and the immensity of black suffering on the shores of the New World. Although Gabriel is a cad, he seems steadfast even if the god he worships appears not to be. Gabriel, Baldwin writes, "would not turn his face from God, no matter how deep might grow the darkness in which God hid His face from him." But even as Gabriel refuses to reject "the power of redemption," and fervently seeks after a god who actively conceals its presence from him and his people, we can only speculate about the course his life might have followed in the face of his stubborn belief in this silent god.[4] But based on the life of David Baldwin, the young Baldwin's father, the sense of divine rejection depicted in the fictional life of Gabriel could only lead to the eventual fate the elder Baldwin faced in the real world outside of that imagined for Gabriel in fiction. David, a stalwart old preacher from New Orleans, who appeared in his son's imagination as a "tribal chieftain" and a "prophet in . . . close communion with the Lord," ends his days in bitter madness. After a life of intense struggle, continued deprivation, and diminishing possibilities, David finds himself, his son writes, in a Long Island hospital bed "shriveled and still, like a little black monkey." There, David Baldwin, "eaten up by paranoia" and "locked up in his [own] terrors," was condemned to a prison of insanity that eventually culminated in a lonely death.[5]

Even as a believer and boy minister, the young James Baldwin never seemed to share the unquestioning belief in God's existence and care that his father or his father's fictional counterpart did. Rather, Baldwin from the very start was deeply suspicious of the nature and existence of God. The two male characters in Baldwin's fiction that most mirror their creator, John in *Go Tell It* and Leo Proudhammer in *Tell Me How Long the Train's Been Gone,* closely match Baldwin's own sentiments in that they do not hesitate to question and even curse God's existence. Before his conversion, midway through the novel, John observes a noisy church meeting filled with the rhythmic incantations of prayer and praise and pointedly questions the efficacy of all the intense religious feeling. The young John asks, "why did they come here" to call out to a "God who cared nothing for them—if, above this flaking ceiling, there was any God at all?"[6] Leo Proudhammer, a Baldwin-like celebrity and actor who appears in Baldwin's little-noticed *Tell Me How Long,* published in 1968, dramatizes even more spectacularly than John Baldwin's refusal to accept God's apparent silence. Daring God to stop an incestuous relationship he intends to consummate with his brother to comfort him, Leo taunts God, challenging God as he denounces the deity as the "greatest coward in the universe." Hearing nothing from God in response, Baldwin's Leo continues to rain curses on his silent interlocutor and mocks a supposedly watchful deity as he consummates the relationship. In his monologue, heard only by God (and us), a mocking Leo shouts, "I hoped that God was watching. He probably was. He never did anything else." Proclaiming that he does not fear this impotent god "who took all and gave nothing," Leo asserts that consummating his relationship would provide healing only he could give. Convinced of this peculiar remedy, Leo ends his unorthodox prayer with a defiance mixed with tenderness for his brother. "I'll love you Caleb, I'll love you forever," Leo says, and in the sight of God and the world, "I'll sing hallelujahs to my love for you in hell."[7]

John and Leo echo the voice of their creator, James Baldwin, whose memories of his short history in the church were laced with "the unspeakable pain" of his terror-filled conversion experience. It was as if, remembering that conversion, Baldwin tells us in *Fire,* "I were yelling up to Heaven and Heaven would not hear me."[8] And so, like many of his fictional characters, Baldwin struggled with great difficulty to see how a caring god could exist in a world weighed down with the ever present reality of suffering. When Baldwin writes how God "would not hear me," he suggests that God might have been able to answer his petition but for whatever reason refused. It is an active, divine disregard and not God's impotence and apparent irrelevance that finally push Baldwin to leave the faith. In some of his early fiction, published in his high school magazine before he left the ministry and the church, Baldwin dramatizes the loss of faith he himself experiences. In one short story, "Peace on Earth," Baldwin through his characters manages to question the validity of religious belief without quite rejecting it. The setting for the story is war and combat. John, the protagonist, invokes biblical poetry and pleads with God for safety from the raining bullets and exploding shells. When a comrade dies, the contradiction at the heart of Christianity and all monotheistic faiths is plainly expressed in a question the narrator, Scotty, asks: "why is there no peace on earth? Christ came to bring peace." And despite Baldwin's attempt to answer this question, the divine presence he offers the reader is more promised than realized. Peace for Baldwin's characters is always close but never fully present. And John toward the end of this short story shares with his comrades the highly provisional character and promise of divine reality. "Christ would never be recognized," Johns says, "until the sky cracked and the earth trembled with the power and glory of His return."[9]

As Baldwin's impatience grows, the provisional nature of divine reality does not remain compelling. Several months later, in another short story about wartime combat, entitled "Incident in London," Baldwin moves away from the tentative expressions of faith found in "Peace on Earth" to dramatize the actual loss of faith itself. The brief story begins with a soldier who approaches a religious edifice—"a small chapel" on a "white still street." The chapel represents Baldwin's notion of religion as a "thing," he writes, "eternal, a bulwark and a refuge from strife and from fear." It is a beacon "in the dim, frosty moonlight" that draws the young solider in and demonstrates how religion maintains its allure for both the solider and the author. But at the story's climax, even as the solider hurries toward it, the chapel "crumbles" and collapses presumably from a round of gunfire moments after he has entered the worship space and knelt in prayer beneath a cross. "And suddenly the skies blazed fire," Baldwin writes, "and the stars were blotted out, and a roar of fury filled the universe." The story concludes suddenly with the unceremonious death of the solider and the realization that the chapel and the religion it symbolizes could no longer maintain the pretense of holiness separate from the muck of earthly existence; despite all, it could not ward off the finality of death. "[T]he chapel had been destroyed," Baldwin concludes, "and the snow was no longer pure, but filthy." In the face of a cruel universe full of the bombs and bullets of war, religion, Baldwin suggests, simply "crumbles" beneath the weight of untold suffering, the chaos of the outside world, and the inevitability of death. Midway through the story, Baldwin describes how the solider lost his faith, and in his description we see the fading of Baldwin's own faith as well. As Baldwin writes, "He [the solider] had believed in God, in peace, in righteousness, and the dignity and decency of man. But after he had fought, and had seen how strife degraded and destroyed humanity, his faith had lost its glory and had disappeared."[10]

This image of an attractive, imaginary religious world undone by the suffering and chaos of war should not obscure the genuine attachment Baldwin once had with the holiness church culture of his youth. Even though Baldwin himself sometimes portrayed his teenage ministry as a fraudulent, manipulative hustle of what he knew to be false, his boyhood friends and his mother consistently portrayed him as sincere in his religious hope. The young Jimmy they knew was honest and fervent in his religious beliefs and in his earnest desire to be a preacher. Berdis Baldwin, recalling when her son told her "there's nothing I want to do more than be a preacher," recounted her own reaction to Baldwin biographer Fern Eckman. She said, "I was really surprised. I was shocked. It wasn't a common thing to preach so young. And he was so shy. But I knew he was sincere."[11] Arthur Moore, a boyhood friend who first accompanied him to Mother Horn's church, attested to how "devout" the young Jimmy was. He attended church services several times a week and abstained from worldly vices like smoking, movies, and dancing.[12] But despite his apparent sincerity, what Baldwin's early teenage stories demonstrate is how intensely he struggled with his religious heritage as a young writer. The religion bequeathed to him on the threshing floor of Mother Horn's church was uneasily won and quickly lost.

Even though Baldwin was once a sincere believer, the depth of human suffering and the extent to which his allegiance to holiness church culture cut him off from his artistic impulses strained and eventually severed his commitment to the institutional church. Even so, surrounded with humanity's evident depravity, Baldwin, like the solider he described in "Incident in London," is still drawn toward the chapel and the attractive illusory world of religion. Looking at nature and history, Baldwin has determined that the universe "has made no room" for black people. In near despair, Baldwin looks to religious resources to uphold his sense of fairness. As Baldwin writes: "And if one despairs—as who has not?—of human love, God's love alone is left." But Baldwin finds no answers to the ceaseless questions he hurls at the heavens. Baldwin hears only God's apparent silence before the suffering of black people "cast down so low." And as Baldwin bemoans, speaking of his conversion: "I found no answer on the floor—not *that* answer, anyway—and I was on the floor all night." Baldwin suggests that the only way he could have avoided sharing his father's fate of insanity and death was to question and even curse the silent Christian god of his father and leave the church. But the Christian god he depicts is not only silent; he is also white and malevolent. Baldwin confesses that despite himself, "unwillingly" he knew even as he found himself on "that tremendous floor" during his conversion that God "is white."[13] Before this white god, Baldwin achieves his manhood. But in the end, Baldwin's hopes for eternal glory are shattered before the seemingly permanent reality of black suffering. Any promise he initially found in the faith of his youth was undermined by the betrayal of a god who was not only silent but also hostile to the life chances of black people and their own sense of worth.

A White God's Malevolence and the Empty Promise of Conversion

In the scope of Baldwin's work, the reality of a white malevolent god begins on "that tremendous floor" of Mother Horn's church. There, the young Harlem writer had a conversion experience that he later characterized as the aggressive invasion of his body and psyche by an external and seemingly divine presence. "The Outing," a short story published before *Go Tell It*, and with many of the same characters, is perhaps the first instance in Baldwin's writing where he describes God's spirit in strongly aggressive terms. In this story about the members of the Mount of Olives Pentecostal Assembly and their outing during Independence Day, one leading "saint" assures the many young people on the trip, "You just stay around the house of God long enough . . . [and] one of these days the Spirit'll jump on you. I won't forget the day It jumped on me."[14] The hint of aggression suggested in the phrase "jump on you" only becomes more explicit and angrier over time.

In *Go Tell It*, a sense of terror frames both John's anticipation and his eventual participation in the religious practice of conversion and helps readers prepare for the domineering god that appears in the concluding sections of the novel. In this, the novel mirrors the descriptions of spirit possession first found and described in "The Outing." In the novel, as John witnesses an active evening service and prepares unconsciously for the initiation rite of conversion, he begins to feel what Baldwin describes as "a terror he had never felt before."[15] And when the climatic event overtakes him, an aggressive external force overwhelms John. As Baldwin writes,

> And something moved in John's body which was not John. He was invaded, set at naught, possessed. This power had struck John, in the head or in the heart; and in a moment wholly, filling him with an anguish that he could never in his life have imagined, that he surely could not endure, that even now he could not believe, had opened him up; had cracked him open, as wood beneath the axe cracks down the middle, as rocks break up; had ripped him and felled him in a moment, so that John had not felt the wound, but only the agony, had not felt the fall, but only the fear.[16]

Here, terror not only frames John's understanding of his conversion but also defines the experience itself, not as a moment of joy and celebration but as a moment of "agony" and "fear."

This depiction of an aggressive god who ruthlessly seizes the body and the personality becomes more explicit in Baldwin's later works of nonfiction. In *Fire*, conversion is described as "the anguish that filled me," that moves with a force that could "devastate counties, tearing everything down." Conversion is the "strangest sensation" he has ever had. Baldwin again uses words like *pagan* and *desperate* to depict the basic human responses he experienced on Mother Horn's church floor.[17] The incomprehensible character of evangelical conversion does not simply appear in the act itself but also in how the experience seizes the human personality and lays bare the very essence of an individual's identity. Describing this instant of revelation Baldwin writes in a later essay, "This moment changes one forever. One is confronted with the agony and the nakedness and the beauty of a power which has no end, which contains you, and which you contain, and which will be using you when your bones are dust."[18] Even so, Baldwin's memories about the pervasive sense of ecstasy and power of unexpected revelation are not framed in the language of delight but of pain. In *Fire,* Baldwin confesses that all he really remembers is "the pain, the unspeakable pain."[19]

But as an older Baldwin begins to shape and interpret his memories of that eventful night, his focus on its shock, trauma, and pain give way to a broader perception of the Christian god's disregard and malevolence toward black people. The real trauma begins not with the actual divine encounter but rather with the sharp realization that despite this earth-shattering conversion experience black suffering remains intractable. As Baldwin remembers in *Fire:* "I found no answer on the floor—not *that* answer, anyway—and I was on the floor all night."[20] What may have begun as astonished bewilderment at God's silence is transformed over time into anger at the possibility of God's willful abandonment. For Baldwin, history demonstrates that no matter how traumatic and painful these conversions may have been, they ultimately come to naught. The seizing of the human personality that comes with conversion seems to produce no fundamental good for black people as individuals or collectively. He is "just as black," Baldwin tells us, after the conversion as he was on his day of birth.[21] In future years, of course, desperate to retain the favor of younger radicals enmeshed in the Black Power movement of the late 1960s, Baldwin is very careful never to equate, as he does in the epigraph, blackness with something that needs to be changed.

Despite this, Baldwin does capture something here that would continue to be a touchstone in his later writing in ways that would open cultural space within black culture for the more secular and non-Christian orientations of young black activists and artists of the early 1970s to the present. Leo Proudhammer's cries that taunt God for cowardice capture Baldwin's tone most strikingly. But while it might demonstrate how intensely Baldwin struggled with the white Christian god, it also represents perhaps the final exorcism of God from black fiction and progressive black culture. In Baldwin's wake, Toni Morrison, Ntozake Shange, Alice Walker, Octavia Butler, and other black women writers and artists would create new literary worlds where people are not defined by their ties to Christian concerns and themes. For literary scholar Trudier Harris, Baldwin's *Go Tell It* and Lorraine Hansberry's *Raisin in the Sun* represent "Christianity's last stand" in black literary tradition. As Harris writes: "What would have been blasphemy for Baldwin's characters [in *Go Tell It*] becomes for his descendants a way of creating space for black women to grow, to know and define themselves."[22] Presumably this growth might extend not just beyond the institutional confines of Christianity but beyond its symbolic world as well. So, while this white Christian god, after the tumultuous sixties, might have been exiled from much of progressive black culture, it still helps to shape and define the Harlem-born writer. Baldwin may suggest that this god has proved to be powerless to effect any real amelioration of suffering, but at least it has the power to haunt Baldwin's dreams and nearly every page of his later work — both fiction and nonfiction.

Like his fictional creation Leo Proudhammer, as late as the early 1980s, Baldwin asserted that given the depth of black suffering during the mass enslavement of African peoples and its aftermath, God must be deeply racist. Ernest Champion reports on Baldwin's "respectful repartee" with a Catholic nun and priest near a college where Baldwin was teaching and lecturing. While the two religious largely concurred with Baldwin's invectives against the failings of the church and other religious institutions, they refused to concede to Baldwin's "insistent claim that God appeared somehow or other to be biased, indeed racist."[23] To the extent that a supernatural external God continues to have a place in Baldwin's published work, the Christian deity is consistently depicted as angry and malevolent. From Baldwin's perspective, God emerges from the collective imagination and springs most directly from humanity's fundamental mistrust of nature and society's attempt to regulate human sexuality and behavior through external symbols and sanctions.

Of course, the broader question that emerges is whether dramatic conversions necessarily promote a false consciousness that constrains the possibilities for self-actualization in black communities and contributes to the continued subjugation of black women and men. In challenging the validity of god-talk, Baldwin, consciously or not, participates in a much larger tradition among black people in the United States who have challenged theistic assumptions of the Afro-Protestant consensus forged right after the Civil War. While there is no evidence of any connection with Nella Larsen, a woman writer of mixed racial heritage during the Harlem Renaissance, Baldwin's efforts in *Go Tell It* echoes Larsen's work done decades earlier. In a scene from her book *Quicksand*, published in 1928, the female protagonist undergoes a conversion experience that seems to anticipate Baldwin's later depiction of young John's experience in *Go Tell It*. When the beleaguered Helga, of mixed African and Dutch ancestry, wanders with "no definite destination" into a late-night service at a black revivalist church in Harlem, Larsen describes the setting with sexually charged language brimming with physicality strikingly similar to Baldwin's account of John's conversion. Immediately as Helga walks in she sees "the writhings and weepings" of "frenzied women" who gesticulate, scream, and cry to cadences set by a chanting preacher. But as Helga stands transfixed by the spectacle before her, fascination transforms into near terror. As Larsen writes: "Helga Crane watched until there crept upon her an indistinct horror of an unknown world. She felt herself in the presence of a nameless people, observing rites of a remote obscure origin." And when she finally succumbs to "an echo of the weird orgy" in her heart, she explodes. Capturing the moment, Larsen writes, "Maddened, she grasped at the railing, and with no previous intention began to yell like one insane, drowning every other clamor, while torrents of tears streamed down her face."[24]

Larsen's portrayal of Helga is remarkably similar to Baldwin's account of John. Both authors use sexually charged language to convey the physical expressiveness of religious ecstasy, while their protagonists' conversions are framed within a context of an "indistinct horror" from which they cannot escape. But beyond these similarities, later passages in Larsen's *Quicksand* demonstrate a parallel view of religion that defines it as an illusory, defensive shield that wards off the danger and suffering of an unfair world. When Helga is finally overcome, Larsen describes how her moment of conversion meets her intense need for comfort, simplicity, and a refuge. "[A] miraculous calm came upon her," Larsen writes, and "life seemed to expand, and to become very easy . . . and to the kneeling girl time seemed to sink back into the mysterious grandeur and holiness of far-off simpler centuries."[25] Larsen, like Baldwin years later, also describes the empty promise at the root of conversion-brokered religion. For her, conversion is a form of false consciousness through which patriarchy is expressed and enacted. In Larsen's story, religion entraps Helga in an exploitative marriage with a minister who impregnates her over and over again without regard for her wishes or her safety. And after a particularly difficult and precarious childbirth, Helga comes to a revelation that Baldwin's characters never fully achieve. As Larsen writes: "The cruel, unrelieved suffering had beaten down her protective wall of artificial faith in the infinite wisdom, in the mercy of God. For had she not called in her agony on Him? And He had not heard. Why? Because, she knew now, He wasn't there. Didn't exist." Larsen also, like Baldwin years later, condemns this nonexistent Christian god as "a white man's God."[26]

Even given these similarities, Larsen goes significantly further than Baldwin in suggesting that religious conversion is a form of false consciousness. In Baldwin's case, however, his description of conversion and religious rhetoric is freighted with much more ambivalence and reveals the fissures within black evangelical culture much more clearly than Larsen ever could. Baldwin seems more determined to hold on to the religious rituals of his parents. They are not just an expression of false consciousness but they are also an expression of verve, passion, and vivacious black life. Like Larsen's Helga, Baldwin rejects any notion of a loving, supernatural god even while he maintains an admiration for the love ethic and the musical energies of the black Christian church that worships this kind of god. Where Larsen dispenses entirely with a god, Baldwin replaces the mythical loving god of old with a malevolent one that actively and personally bedevils him.

Again, Leo Proudhammer, as presented in what one biographer calls Baldwin's "most self-conscious" book, *Tell Me How Long,* announces a more fully realized perspective from Baldwin that only begins to emerge with *Fire* and demonstrates his deeply conflicted position on God's presence.[27] Baldwin's Leo essentially seems to dramatize his creator's own internal conflict when he storms within himself: "No, I had had quite enough of God—more than enough, more than enough, the horror filled my nostrils, on the blood-drenched name; and yet was forced to see that this horror, precisely, accomplished His reality and undid my unbelief."[28] As one Baldwin scholar notes, the real meaning of Leo's anguished words actually put him "in the paradoxical position of the apparent atheist whose disbelief is so strong that it means the contrary."[29] Baldwin's characters would never say what Larsen's do. As Larsen's Helga on one occasion says to herself: "She couldn't, she thought ironically, even blame God for it now that she knew that He didn't exist."[30] But while Larsen is willing to extinguish God's presence from Helga's inner world, Baldwin and his literary creations appear prepared to leave God in place to hate.

"Improbable Aristocrats": The Moral Superiority of Redemptive Suffering

Even as he continued in the early 1960s to reject the existence of a loving deity who cares for black people and other members of the dispossessed, Baldwin still saw the redemptive possibilities of suffering. In 1962, Baldwin wrote in the *New Yorker* (later published as part of *The Fire Next Time*) about young black men and women across the South who faced, with nonviolent resistance, white mobs protesting their entrance in public schools and universities. Baldwin describes these quiet young activists as "improbable aristocrats—the only genuine aristocrats this country has produced." In a republic without royalty, Baldwin portrays these young people as achieving their noble status from their arduous struggles against American racism. In "hewing out the mountain of white supremacy," Baldwin claims they achieved their distinctiveness — "the stone of their individuality."[31] In describing an improbable aristocracy of suffering and struggle, Baldwin's rendering runs parallel to how suffering has shaped black religion's evolution in the United States. Black religion's emphasis on suffering begins with how black people have identified with suffering figures from the Hebrew Bible and the New Testament. "[T]he Negro identifies himself almost wholly with the Jew." This identification, according to Baldwin, extends to the New Testament primarily in the "image of the suffering Christ," where Christ is "wedded" to the image of the "suffering Jew" and "the suffering slave" as part of one indivisible moral vision.[32]

But even while Baldwin emphasizes the importance of suffering in this moral vision, he rejects god-talk. Instead, Baldwin adopts language suggestive of twentieth-century nontheistic existentialism. His rhetoric, especially in *Fire*, is imbued with the tragic dimensions of life as he ruminates on the indisputable reality of death and the importance of individual decision in the face of this reality. Baldwin argues that we should "rejoice in the *fact* of death" and decide to "earn" our death by negotiating life with nobility, risk, and courage. In a striking concluding passage of *Fire*, Baldwin defines the history of African Americans as decisively shaped by black people's "endless struggle" for "human identity" in the context of "death and humiliation" and elaborates on his own distinctive moral vision. Baldwin writes:

> I do not mean to be sentimental about suffering but people who cannot suffer can never grow up, can never discover who they are. That man who is forced each day to snatch his manhood, his identity, out of the fire of human cruelty that rages to destroy it knows, if he survives his effort, and even if he does not survive it, something about himself and human life that no school on earth—and, indeed, no church—can teach. He achieves his own authority, and that is unshakable.[33]

This existentialist sensibility colors Baldwin's early critical reflections on white identity in the United States, even as it shapes his understanding of black identity in America. Baldwin manages to keep his focus on black suffering in ways that highlight the hollow center at the core of white identity. For Baldwin, whiteness is a social identity rooted in a god-complex where people desperately avoid death as they deny their own mortality and fear of black people.[34] Baldwin's language is so suggestive and provocative not only because of his criticism of white Americans but also because of the way his focus on suffering defines and illuminates black dignity.

Just a week after the church bombing in Birmingham in 1963 that killed four girls and injured scores of others, Baldwin, in language that echoed what he had written in the *New Yorker* several months before continued to confer a kind of aristocracy on black Americans in a recorded conversation with well-known Christian ethicist Reinhold Niebuhr. In their discussion just after the church bombing and years of racial bombing and violent intimidation, Reinhold Niebuhr and Baldwin mused about "the missing face of Christ." They pondered the possible symbolic meaning of a surviving stain-glass window portrait in the Sixteenth Street Baptist Church of a crucified Jesus with his face knocked out by the blast. For both speakers the missing face represented a malady: established churches' relative inaction in the face of the tumultuous struggle against segregation during the 1950s and 1960s. It also represented the opportunity, as Baldwin saw it, "to give him [Jesus] a new face" and "make hope of Christian love a reality" in the world. Baldwin was frustrated by the church's inability to express true Christian love, but he could not help seeing the civil rights movement as a chance for black people to enact the redemption of a United States founded on the notion of freedom. How "ironic" is it, Baldwin asks Niebuhr during their exchange, "that people who are enslaved . . . are the only hope this country has." They are the "only hope," Baldwin suggests, because they have suffered enough to "discover what they really live by," even as most (white) Americans are caught up in a crass consumerism, where they worry more about "Coca-Cola" than the issues of social justice. Suffering foists a sense of responsibility on black people that many whites have been able to avoid.

During their conversation, Niebuhr, from a perspective of Christian realism, described the ongoing crisis over civil rights as dividing those "who want to be pure" from those "who want to be responsible."[35]

Throughout the sixties, Baldwin would mirror Niebuhr's distinctions in analyzing the position of white people in American society. Increasingly, Baldwin would see white people as those who seek their own purity over justice and avoid responsibility and suffering through privileges gained through their white skin. It is from this perspective that Baldwin would view his many white liberal friends, who were mostly locked out of his "improbable aristocracy" of suffering that so many of African descent have had to join through no choice of their own. For Baldwin, suffering separates the worthy from the unworthy. And so even in the wake of the church bombings in Birmingham, suffering holds purpose even if God does not. On occasion, Baldwin would use a kind of god-talk. Toward the end of his life, while he was teaching at Bowling Green University, a student asked whether he believed in God. Baldwin answered, "My dear, I believe that nothing happens by accident. I believe that my coming to Bowling Green was not an accident. If for a moment I give in to the belief that all life is an accident, then for me life becomes intolerable. There is and always has been a purpose and meaning to life."[36] In general, however, as Willie Walker offers in his recent dissertation, Baldwin "displaces God" and exchanges the deity beyond nature for the power of love as expressed in bodily hu tionships that form a basis from which to help save one another."[37]

In a speech in San Francisco, in October of 1960, before a young college audience, Baldwin spoke about the writer's role in American life and articulated a vision where the potential of human relationships replaces God in the role of creation. At the close of his speech, Baldwin ended with this benediction: "It [the world] will not be transformed by an act of God, but by all of us, by you and me. I don't believe any longer that we can afford to say that it is entirely out of our hands. We made the world we're living in and we have to make it over."[38] Here and elsewhere Baldwin's reflections on suffering and God are imbued with a language of individualism that mirrors his embrace of an existentialist moral posture. As D. Quentin Miller notes in a recent collection of essays on the writer: Baldwin moves from the ultimate expression of external authority—God—to the broader community collectively and individually.[39] Whether individual, personal relationships can contain the collective social vision Baldwin wanted to achieve is debatable. His political vision may not have been robust enough for a large and complicated world. But for Baldwin, the individual decisions made in relationships of love against a prevailingly loveless culture could be crucial and even decisive.

One way some Baldwin scholars have struggled to see a larger social vision in Baldwin's work is with the notion of redemptive suffering. In many ways, this notion is a natural extension of Baldwin's aristocracy of suffering. Michael Lynch in several articles explores religious themes in Baldwin's novels and attempts to demonstrate the importance of redemptive suffering in Baldwin's moral vision. From a father's illness and death that sparks self-discovery in both his clergy wife and son (as in *The Amen Corner*), to a despondent friend's suicide that illuminates the nature of his companions' lives (as in Baldwin's 1961 novel *Another Country*), Lynch describes how suffering works as a redemptive force in Baldwin's fiction. In Baldwin's imaginative worlds, suffering often prompts the self-examination necessary for love to flourish. And this love becomes the principal site for transformation and self-actualization.[40]

The principal way Baldwin envisions redemptive suffering as part of a broader political vision is in the arena of artistic creativity. For Baldwin, suffering is intrinsic to the creative process. As Lynch writes: "Baldwin suggests that art is the hope and the strength of the person who recognizes the inevitability of suffering and who manages to transform that experience into a form which somehow transcends affliction."[41] So despite gestures toward a nebulous notion of divine providence in his novels and some of his recorded conversations, Baldwin seems hesitant to go beyond the interpersonal realm in his efforts to rescue meaning from a world that has so much suffering. Instead, he considers suffering's role in creativity in very individualistic terms. And since suffering and pain tends to atomize groups and isolate individuals who must confront their own personal limits and mortality, it is not surprising that in some ways Baldwin's vision undermines any real attempt to construct a broader societal notion of redemptive suffering from his writings. Baldwin, instead, bases his stories of pain on his own autobiography. With a surefooted-ness that sometimes eludes him when he attempts to delineate a larger political vision, Baldwin throughout his work traffics in the personal realm of small hurts and big bruises that mark most ordinary human relationships. Baldwin asserts that writers cannot separate "the things that hurt" from "the things which helped him [or her]."[42]

Although many may link Baldwin's notions of suffering's redemptive value with traditional theological notions of the atoning work of Christ's crucifixion, the grand visions of redemptive suffering still seem misplaced. They overwhelm Baldwin's fragile excavation of the dangers and tender joys of love. It is this love that pushes him in part to reject the cry for judgment at the core of his father's apocalyptic religion. But even as Baldwin rejects the parochialism inherent in the judgment rhetoric of evangelicalism, his vision of an aristocracy of sufferers, in fact, betrays the extent to which he retains some relationship with the evangelical perspective of his youth. Like his father, Baldwin sees hope for a righteous few in the ultimate damnation of those (white elites) who have demonstrated their moral inferiority through their own acts of brutality. He embraces the strategies of a religious perspective he seemingly rejects as he envisages suffering as the key in the development of black people's gift to the United States and to humanity in the rhythms and music of the blues. Suffer-ing in this view is as constitutive to all forms of creativity as it is to human life itself. Even as he acknowledges it as the very creative stuff of life, Baldwin makes no serious claims for suffering as fitted to an unseen providential scheme. As Luke tells his son in *The Amen Corner:* "Son—don't try to get away from the things that hurt you—sometimes that's all you got. You got to learn to live with those things—and use them. I've seen people—put themselves through terrible torture—and die because they were afraid of getting hurt."[43]

The creative artistic life then, from this perspective, is birthed from lives lived with risk where people refuse to stay in a safe cocoon of self-declared moral purity but instead plunge ahead, making music and song in the danger-ous mire of a profane world. In Baldwin's godless world, suffering is not inher-ently good or redemptive. Pain and suffering, instead, are fitted however inequitably among us into the very fabric of human existence. The broadly encompassing nature of human suffering makes it foolish to deny its presence or live as if it could be escaped. And since suffering cannot be avoided, it can provide some context for a response that harnesses that human adaptability that sometimes surfaces in the midst of hardship. Pain becomes the stage from which a fierce will can achieve self-creation.

Leo, flush with anger over the burdens of his racial identity during an acting audition, speaks early in *Tell Me How Long* about the role of pain in the creative life in ways that echo Baldwin's language in *Fire*. For Leo explains that only his human will could possibly invest pain with "coherence and an authority." And from this foundation Leo believes he gains the chance for creativity and self-creation. As Leo recognizes the universal character of suffering, he begins to assess his opportunities and "this possibility of creating my language out of my pain, of using my pain to create myself." Leo determines that "pain was the horse that I must learn to ride."[44] Suffering becomes the ultimate context for the achievement of black manhood in much of Baldwin's fiction.[45] When Vivaldo and his close friend and sometime lover Eric in an earlier novel, *Another Country*, discuss whether it is "admirable" to feel pain, Vivaldo answers, "I think that perhaps you can begin to *become* admirable." Perhaps, Vivaldo concludes, "if you can accept the pain that almost kills you, you can use it, you can become better."[46]

It is from this perspective that Baldwin sees the development of the blues and other forms of black music. For Baldwin, this music essentially serves to "invest" black pain with coherence and create a language crucial for the creation of an independent healthy black self that opposes a broader culture steeped in the ideals of white supremacy. Clearly, Baldwin believes in the transforming power of music and other art forms. They have captured his imagination and ambitions since the beginning. For Baldwin, the creation of black music from black suffering like the blues, the spirituals, and gospels uncover a dignity in the lives of black people not unlike the nobility of landed sovereigns.

The Collapse of Moral Aristocracy: Martin King's Death and the Anguish-Laden Blues

While Leo, Baldwin's literary twin in *Tell Me How Long*, auditions for an acting company remarkably like the famous Actors Studio of the 1960s, he flirts with a young woman "with real eyes in a real face." Her sudden presence at the piano where he has retreated offers a welcome respite from his overwrought state and his recent descent into self-pity and thoughts of suicide. He stops musing about how unfair racism is and begins, instead, to play the blues for the young woman he is flirting with. "I'll try to sing a blues for you," Leo says to the young woman, "and, after that, even if I'm asked to leave, if you've liked it,

I won't mind exile at all."[47] For Baldwin, as this scene suggests, the blues captured the ability of black people to wrest meaning and purpose from anguish even in the midst of exile. The blues is a key example, for Baldwin, of how suffering can be the context for artistic production and partial redemption. It functions as a balm for a weary people exiled from a home to which they can never return and helps to make burdensome life bearable. It is the simple act of singing the blues that helps Leo not to "mind" both the real and inner exile he feels as a black person in the United States.

In an earlier short piece for *Playboy* entitled "The Uses of Blues," Baldwin anticipates these explorations in *Tell Me How Long*, and he celebrates the blues as a "uniquely *American* art form" and as a decisive metaphor for the black struggle for freedom in the United States. As Baldwin discusses the title for this essay written for *Playboy*, he defines the blues as a state of being rather than simply as a musical form. The blues refers "to the experience of life, or the state of being, out of which the blues come." He explains that he might have entitled his brief essay "The Uses of Anguish" or "The Uses of Pain," but he decided "to talk about the blues, not only because they speak of this particular experience of life and this state of being but because they contain the toughness that manages to make this experience articulate."[48] Of course in highlighting blues music's expressiveness and how it speaks of a "particular experience of life" where pain is commonplace, Baldwin bargains that there are people outside of the black community who will listen intently and learn about the experience the blues make "articulate." With the assassination of Martin King, Baldwin begins to doubt whether any powerful person in white society hears what those who play and sing the blues are trying to say.

So despite Baldwin's continued praise of the power of the blues and its connection to black lives of struggle, King's death in 1968 forced Baldwin to rethink how suffering could possibly be redemptive. He began to wonder whether suffering truly conferred a moral aristocracy to those who experience it in unequal measure. With King's murder, Baldwin could no longer claim, without some very significant qualifications, that suffering had redemptive power in the face of those who may willfully and sadistically perpetrate violence on nonviolent activists struggling for economic and racial justice. King's death changed everything. "[T]he manner of his death," Baldwin confesses in one essay, "has forced me into a judgment concerning human life and human beings, which I have always been reluctant to make."[49] In a conversation with John Hall in 1970, Baldwin stated quite plainly the nature of his shift in attitude, and Hall was startled when Baldwin declared the death of the civil rights movement. As Baldwin explained, "Well, we've marched and petitioned for a decade, and now it's clear that there's no point in marching or petitioning."[50]

For Baldwin, when the assassin killed King, he killed the hope that "the conscience of a nation" could be reached through protest and petition. What died with the assassin's bullet in Memphis was not the eternal dream for equality but rather Baldwin's (and others') faith in white people's ability to change and answer, based on our collective humanity, the petitions of those oppressed. Baldwin once had much more hope for the promise of America. But after the brutal slaying of the central apostle of nonviolence and reconciliation in the United States, Baldwin declared that no one could "be deluded by [presumably white] Americans anymore."[51]

Baldwin, never entirely comfortable with the label of integrationist for himself, saw more and more merit in the arguments of black cultural and religious nationalists. With King's murder, Baldwin's thinking mirrored the shift evident throughout many black communities, particularly among young people, as the Black Power movement of the late 1960s became ascendant over the techniques of nonviolent action and petition King had long advocated. Baldwin now accented black agency instead of relying on pricking a seemingly dormant white conscience. Given this white intransigence, Baldwin saw the value of black self-reliance. He had long shared the suspicions of black nationalists who saw the very definition of America as built on black subjugation—black labor. But despite this kinship, Baldwin would never advocate a truly revolutionary separatism because of his deep attachment and even love of all things American. His relationship with his home country was a pained one marked with a palpable disappointment in the white liberal friends who had long been his patrons. As Baldwin writes, "A person does not lightly elect to oppose his society. One would much rather be at home among one's compatriots than be mocked and detested by them." But along with his desire for justice and freedom for black people, Baldwin, despite himself, finds that he is "helpless" before his love of country.[52]

But despite this love (or perhaps because of it), increasingly throughout the sixties Baldwin used the fiery language of judgment to mask his bewildered disappointment at the ignorance of so many of his fellow (white) citizens; he knew that unless they changed their course, American society would be in danger of self-destructing. In *No Name in the Street,* Baldwin grapples with his disappointment in white people's capacity for self-delusion and their remarkable reluctance to engage in self-reflection even in the face of self-destructive impulses. If they were not so "terrified of their private selves," Baldwin suggests they would not need "to invent" what they call "the Negro problem." Writing in 1972 just a few years after King's murder, Baldwin tells his white liberal audience that it is white people who have created the race problem. They invented it with their "guilty and constricted white imagination" in order to "safeguard their purity," and in the process they have made themselves the true "criminals" and "monsters," not the black men and women they fear. Black people become the "scapegoats" who pay "for the sins of others." But now after King's death, the scapegoat myth—the myth of redemptive suffering—is no longer compelling for Baldwin. No matter how much "the scapegoat may be made to suffer, his suffering cannot purify the sinner," Baldwin warns. The scapegoat, instead, "merely incriminates" and "seals" the "damnation" of white oppressors.[53]

So after King's death, Baldwin can no longer see the suffering of black people as redemptive for a nation that constricts the life chances of black people while continuing to kill their moral leaders. In Baldwin's eyes the myth of redemptive suffering—of the scapegoat—is bankrupt; only blood is left. Although the scapegoat has resulted "in seas of blood," in fact "not one sinner as been saved, or changed, by this despairing ritual."[54] Baldwin, instead, sees the continued enormity of black suffering as merely an indictment of white Americans—an indictment that will last seemingly into eternity. As Baldwin writes: "[T]he failure and betrayal are in the record book forever, and sum up, and condemn, forever, those descendants of a barbarous Europe who arbitrarily and arrogantly reserve the right to call themselves Americans." The moral aristocracy conferred by suffering died with Martin King. After "seas of blood" had been shed, there can be no redemption; there is only the indictment of an accusing finger directed at those more concerned with "their purity" than their "private selves." Describing the impact of King's death Baldwin says simply, "something has altered in me, something has gone away."[55]

"And That's True Religion": Healing and the Partial Redemption of Music

Despite everything, what Baldwin found, from his earliest days to the moments of despair he experienced after King's death, is that songs of praise were more compelling to him than any philosophical pronouncements about the nature of God's existence and presence in creation. For Baldwin, suffering truly shaped and defined black musical forms from blues to gospel as genuine artistic expressions that demonstrate the redemptive possibilities of suffering and often convey a sense of divine presence. In *Go Tell It* Baldwin demonstrates how central music is in his artistic imagination as it conveys both the presence of God and the dignity of human beings. John, in fact, glimpses the sacred even before his climatic conversion at the end of the novel through the music he hears played and sung during a late-night prayer meeting. As Baldwin writes, "Their singing caused him to believe in the presence of the Lord; indeed, it was no longer a question of belief, because they made that presence real."[56] So, to the extent that John (and perhaps Baldwin) feel a positive divine presence at all, it is not from creedal affirmations but rather from the communal efforts of song and praise that help, in fact, to give reality and shape to God.

The harsher language toward organized religion in *The Amen Corner* masks, to some degree, how Baldwin still finds church music compelling even after he leaves the ministry. To the extent that the black holiness church has any energy and allure for Baldwin it is because of its music. As literary scholar Saadi Simawe writes in a strong analysis of the importance of music in Baldwin's play: "To Baldwin, who is naturally allergic to ideologies, music in *The Amen Corner* becomes the only religion worth practicing primarily because it lends full expression to the deepest human desire and feeling."[57] Simawe persuasively analyzes how Baldwin enfolds the entire production of his first produced play in music. Music introduces the play, and it adds punctuation and texture throughout. From the very beginning, Baldwin connects the gospel rhythms to the blues. In his opening stage instructions he directs that the musical prologue, "The Blues Is Man" segue "into a steady rollicking beat" for the spiritual the congregation initially will sing to invoke the presence of the Christian god. These initial instructions indicate how central music will be in the play and in the church's continued influence over its people. Baldwin instructs the producers of the play to place David's piano that plays both the blues and gospel "under everything" on stage with the church overhanging in the apartment below. For Baldwin this overhanging position of the church was, as his directions indicate, to "give the impression of dominating the family's living quarters." At the same time, it is the music more than anything else that provides the energies on which the church's power rests. No matter how important and prominent the Bible or preaching is in Margaret's church, the placement of David's piano "under everything" demonstrates how central music will be for every person on stage. Music dominates not only the living quarters, as Baldwin's stage directions suggest, but the lives of everyone at church and at home.[58]

The power of the blues, so evident in *The Amen Corner*, is also interwoven into the very structure of much of Baldwin's later work of the 1970s. Baldwin celebrates the importance of the blues in *Just Above My Head*, initially published in 1979. In this, Baldwin's last novel, blues achieves a kind of sacred status. Where *The Amen Corner* in its original set and thematic structure merely suggests the underlying importance of music and its true place as religion's animating force, Hall Montana, the central narrator in *Just Above My Head*, clearly affirms the role the rhythms of church song play. As Hall speculates: "Maybe all gospel songs begin out of blasphemy and presumption—what the church would call blasphemy and presumption: out of entering God's suffering and challenging God Almighty to have or to give or to withhold mercy."[59] All at

once, Baldwin locates music on the very outer boundaries of institutional religion and connects it to suffering he believes is key to artistic creativity and to
his constant challenge of the traditional Christian god.

Beneath Baldwin's often-inflated language of spiritual aristocracies and
the like is recognition that while some possibility for transformation and self-
actualization can be found in the rhythms and sounds of the blues, these possibilities are in fact limited and sometimes just of the moment. In the second act,
midway through *The Amen Corner*, David's father, as a fellow musician com-
pelled to make rhythm, swing, and sound, describes the role and real limits of
music to his son, who believes music is all you need. "Music is a moment,"
Luke cautions David. "But life's a long time."

> In that moment, when it's good, when you really swinging—then you
> joined to everything, to everybody, to skies and stars and every living
> thing. But music ain't kissing. Kissing's what you want to do. Music's
> what you *got* to do, *if* you do it. Question is how long you can keep up
> with the music when you ain't got nobody to kiss. You know, the music
> don't come out of the air, baby. It comes out of the man who's blowing it.[60]

Of course, Baldwin understands how singing and playing the blues confront
both the musicians and their audiences with the pain and suffering of a people.
But Baldwin also understands that this music is not simply the voicing of pain.
Music also helps to create time for love and gives space for intimacy against the
overwhelming odds of a harsh world. While music maintains its potential for
transcendent transformation, Baldwin deliberately scales down how he represents its power to fit within the small tender relationships human beings can
have with one another.

In his short story "Sonny's Blues," initially published in 1957, Baldwin's
embrace of black music and its possibilities flowers in ways only hinted at in his
earlier fiction and plays. It affirms and extends Luke's understanding of the
power of the blues and music generally for personal transformation and healing. This story perhaps represents Baldwin's fullest exploration of the role and
power of music for individual healing and community formation. In this story
about the broken relationship between two brothers, music is sacramental. It
becomes the primary vehicle for a partial reconciliation and the reestablishment
of intimacy. When Sonny, a jazzman battling addiction, invites his brother to a
late-night jam session, the blues, in the words of critic John Reilly, not only
"repairs the relationship between two men" but also "becomes a metaphor" for
the black community.[61]

Throughout his short story, Baldwin once again invokes the language of
religious ritual. Long before Sonny and the narrator find themselves in that
nightclub, Baldwin conveys the power of music through a language suggestive

of religious possibilities. When both brothers witness "an old time revival meet-ing" and a beleaguered group who sing gospel hymns of old on the street cor-ner, Baldwin's description manages to convey the limits and irony of black religious speech better than any of his other works of fiction. As the singers announce how "the old ship of Zion . . . has rescued many a thousand," the nar-rator counters: "Not a soul under the sound of their voices were hearing this song for the first time, not one of them had been rescued." And while the singers sing of a rescue that never comes, Baldwin demonstrates how truly tangled the sacred and profane are in black people's folkways as he portrays the singers as just barely removed from the worldly collection of people they are singing to. "The woman with the tambourine, whose voice dominated the air, whose face was bright with joy," Baldwin writes, "was divided by very little from the woman who stood watching her, a cigarette between her heavy, chapped lips . . . her face scarred and swollen from many beatings." Even as strangers to one another, their similarities allow them to "addres[s] each other as Sister" without strain. The reality that hovers just beyond sight of these soul-ful singers is the deep suffering necessary to produce a music and art that is truly compelling. "When I was . . . listening to that woman sing," Sonny tells his brother, "it struck me all of a sudden how much suffering she must have had to go through—to sing like that."[62]

Despite these fits of irony that hint at music's limitations for promoting broader societal change, Baldwin also manages to convey the power of music to transform within the smaller realm of personal intimacies. Unlike his own conversion where change seemed to come brutally from without, for the city crowd caught outside this makeshift revival in "Sonny's Blues," change is gen-erated from within. As Baldwin writes, "As the singing filled the air the watch-ing listening faces underwent a change, the eyes focusing on something *within;* the music seemed to soothe a poison out of them; and time seemed nearly, to fall away from the sullen belligerent, battered faces, as though they were fleeing back to their first condition, while dreaming their last."[63]

With this marvelous description of music's power, Baldwin prepares his readers for the final scene at the nightclub, where the language of ritual heav-ily intrudes on Baldwin's description of the bandstand. Baldwin describes the way the bandleader, Creole, moves and the way Sonny's performance is initially received with the word *ceremonious.*[64] And indeed, as readers are carried along to the story's conclusion, there is a sense of ceremony and ritual to the pro-ceedings. Readers begin to anticipate the partial reconciliation that does indeed take place between the two brothers just as those who attend evangelical churches anticipate the offer of salvation at the end of service.

This emphasis on ritual helps to explain why some scholars insist that Baldwin simply recasts "the jazz club . . . as a sacred locale" in "Sonny's Blues," transforming the nightspot into a local church with a nearly conventional worship setting.[65] But from the very beginning of Sonny's performance at the club, Baldwin notes how the beleaguered listeners focus on what is "within" instead of on what comes from without. These jazz participants look within themselves and do not expect an external supernatural deity to sanctify their worldly activities of music and drink. What this short story most reveals is that for Baldwin it is music that sanctifies religion and not religion that sanctifies music. This distinction is revealed with particular force during a television conversation between Baldwin and the poet Nikki Giovanni. Midway through their discussion, Baldwin remembers the last time he saw the famous soul singer Aretha Franklin. He excitedly recalls how Franklin performed at the Apollo Theater and turned it "into a gospel church service." Baldwin simply says: "And that's true religion."[66] For Baldwin, it seems, the power associated with true religion does not come with God but with the music sweating, suffering bodies produce—just as true love does.

The pursuit of God and righteousness is often associated with a desire for purity that separates the believer from the muck of the world. But in that nightclub, Sonny, Creole, and the narrator do not seem concerned with staying pure. It is far too late for that. All that is present instead is the suffering intrinsic in all life and the production of much art. As Baldwin writes in the voice of Sonny's brother, the narrator: "I had never before thought of how awful the relationship must be between the musician and his instrument. He has to fill it, this instrument, with the breath of life, his own."[67] Music expresses vivacious life through breath and represents a brash extension of the human will that fills a large space many paces away through notes and beats.

Instead of uselessly raging at a malevolent god, Baldwin focuses here on the sweaty, physical bodies at the root of the love and art he has always celebrated. The restrained hopes offered in these moments seem too small for most institutional forms of religion. When reconciliation begins to come between the two brothers, Baldwin does not invoke God. Instead, he celebrates the arduous human search for physical connection, and beneath the talk about the curse of black suffering, Baldwin ends his reflection on music and the blues with hints of laughter and love. Even as he actively seeks to displace God from an exalted position, he indirectly invokes the sacred with a language deeply suggestive of the rhythms of ritual. As Baldwin begins to restrain his notions of redemptive suffering, he is still left as a kind of theologian of the body without a god. In God's place we find the sweaty bodies that always seem to take center stage in Baldwin's imagination. "Then it was over," Baldwin writes, "Creole and Sonny let out their breath, both soaking wet, and grinning."[68]

Chapter 4

But the Body Was Real

sex, love, and the character
of revelatory experience

I'm not a believer in any sense that would make sense to any church, and any church would obviously throw me out. I believe—what do I believe? I believe in. I believe in love . . . I believe we can save each other.

CONVERSATION WITH COLIN MACINNESS, *1965*

Nikki Giovanni was a young poet of a new rising generation of black artists directly influenced by the Black Power movement of the late 1960s when Baldwin met her in early November of 1971 for a taped conversation in London. Their spirited dialogue about gender relations, race, and the nature of love and religion was recorded for the program "Soul!" and broadcast the following month over the local New York public television station. Early in their conversation the discussion turned to religion and the Christian legend of the Virgin Birth. As always, Baldwin was outraged. "[W]hen you attack it [the Virgin Birth] you're accused of being blasphemous," Baldwin told Giovanni, "[but] I think the legend itself is a blasphemy." Getting more and more exasperated by the moment, Baldwin pressed: "What is wrong with a man and a woman sleeping together, making love to each other and having a baby like everybody else? Why does the son of God have to be born immaculately? Aren't we all the sons of God? That's the blasphemy."[1]

Part of Baldwin's problem with the legend of the Virgin Birth is how it sets one human being above others and seems to absolve human beings of responsibility for their own salvation and their own destiny. In his speech before the WCC, Baldwin rejects the uniqueness of Jesus. And he declares that religious teachings that claim Jesus is the "Son of God" are "a revelation and a revolution," not because he is the sole son of God but because "it means that we are all the sons of God." Because everyone has equal status as children of God, the relationship between Jesus and God is only revelatory when it confirms that all human beings and not just a single pious Jew from Nazareth can claim the divine power necessary to define their own lives. As Baldwin explains, "[W]e are responsible for our soul's salvation, not the bishop, not the priest, not my mother."[2] Even God cannot be held responsible for our salvation because, for Baldwin, God is a human creation. God cannot be responsible for the salvation of human beings, because we as human beings are responsible for God. As Baldwin told Giovanni, with only a touch of humor: "God's only hope is us. If we don't make it, he ain't going to make it either."[3] So, when Baldwin chooses in his own work to dramatize the lowly disreputable birth of a possible savior boy-child, we are not surprised that he refuses to embrace the legend of the Virgin Birth as a blueprint for his new play. In *Blues for Mister Charlie*, his second major play, Baldwin implicitly criticizes the legend, with his brash celebration of sexuality and the breaking of societal taboos. So, although the Virgin Birth's potential exclusivity clearly does not commend the legend to Baldwin, he seems much more concerned in this play with how the story of the Virgin Birth seems to reject the power necessity of physical and sexual intimacy for human fulfillment, love, and new life.

Toward the end of the third act, Juanita, the lover and old childhood sweetheart of a pivotal character, celebrates her pregnancy and the possibility of "one more illegitimate black baby." She and Richard consummate their relationship on his return home after years away, and apparently Juanita conceives during their rendezvous, right before a white racist shopkeeper brutally kills her young beau. This murder—inspired very loosely by the 1955 killing of Emmett Till in Mississippi—is the central act in the play and propels the drama that was first performed in New York in 1964. Juanita, in the wake of Richard's killing, refuses to be ashamed of their premarital sex and its resulting pregnancy. For Juanita, her unborn child not only becomes a symbol of her undying love for Richard, but it also represents her hopes for a man-child to avenge her lover's death. Juanita, mirroring the sentiments of the playwright, sees the acquittal of Richard's killer as a violation of Richard's manhood. And now she relishes how her unborn and hoped-for man-child represents a threat to the larger white society who helped to kill her lover. As Juanita exclaims early in the final act of Baldwin's play: "And I am going to raise my baby to be a man. A *man*, you dig?"[4]

At the same time Juanita celebrates the possibilities of an "illegitimate black baby," she also celebrates her sexuality as she favorably compares her flesh-and-blood lovemaking to her mother's love for God, wryly suggesting, "God does for Mama what Richard did for me." In Juanita, Baldwin draws parallels with the Christian legend of the Virgin Birth. Like the biblical Mary, Juanita sees her pregnancy as one brimming with hope and promise. While Juanita's mother is afraid of what life might hold for her daughter and her new grandson, Juanita holds no such fears. Her "Mama" might be afraid, but this does not prevent Juanita from joyfully exclaiming: "I'm not afraid. I hope I'm pregnant. I *hope* I am!" Juanita even suggests that her lovemaking with Richard was not just similar but superior to any presumed association Mary might have had with the Hebrew god. Juanita desires "a lover made of flesh and blood" and has no desire to be "God's mother." As Juanita proudly proclaims: "I don't want to be God's mother! He can *have* His icy, snow-white heaven."[5] In Baldwin's reenactment of the mythical story of Mary and Joseph in the lives of Juanita and Richard, he fervently embraces sexual connection as a vehicle for love, hope, and promise. Where others might see Baldwin's embrace of sex in *Giovanni's Room, Another Country,* and *Blues for Mister Charlie* as blasphemous, Baldwin sees the schizophrenic denial of sex at the heart of Western culture and the traditional Virgin Birth narrative in Christianity as the truly obscene act. As he told Nikki Giovanni: "The whole heart of the Christian legend . . . impresses me as being really obscene."[6]

The significance of the body and the physical intimacy for Baldwin cannot be overestimated. In his bestseller of 1962, *Another Country,* when considering the fractured marriage of Richard and Cass, Baldwin describes how insufferable the loss of physical tenderness and sexual intimacy can be. Cass, late in the novel, ponders Richard's absence from the marital bed and her own deep craving for any kind of sexual attention. Busy covering up her affair with Richard's longtime friend, Eric, she returns home from a recent outing at a club. Even as Cass, in a cab traveling home, sits terrified at the very thought her husband might find out about her unfaithfulness, she is more troubled by the loss of warmth and intimacy she once shared with her husband. "[T]he loss of intimacy," Cass thinks to herself, "results in the freezing over of the world, and the loss of oneself."[7] Sexual intimacy breaks the chill that falls too often on human relationships and Baldwin's conception of true human intimacy ushers the body back to the center of any critical reflection on the nature of human love. "Despite the fact that sex and love are not the same thing," Baldwin tells Nikki Giovanni, "when a man's sexuality is gone, his possibility, his hope, of loving is also gone."[8] Sex is central to any notion of the human personality and any vision of the self that Baldwin would care to affirm. As he writes in one of his last published essays, "Here Be Dragons," in 1985: "[T]he idea of one's sexuality can only with great violence be divorced or distanced from the idea of the self."[9]

For Baldwin, sexual intimacy holds a sacramental quality as a vehicle for love and truth. In this world, love's emotional territory of human sexual connection replaces the institutional church and reveals risky truths that no one can afford to deny if they want to stay vibrant and alive. According to Baldwin, love exposes our true selves that we sometimes fear to reveal; it is a "state of grace" that involves a "tough and universal sense of quest and daring and growth."[10] In his description of a same-sex relationship between two characters, Eric and Yves, whose love represents the most fully realized relationship in his novel *Another Country*, Baldwin writes: "[T]he act of love is a confession. One lies about the body but the body does not lie about itself; it cannot lie about the force which drives it."[11] In this view love is expansive and active. When challenged about whether his emphasis on love might promote a more passive posture to social change and the world, Baldwin answered in one interview: "I don't mean anything passive. I mean something active, something more like a fire, like the wind, something which can change you."[12] For Baldwin, love is a force that is frighteningly inclusive in its breath and all encompassing in its demands. At the same time, love is an ordinary facet of life; it is among the universal constants in human existence. As "birth, struggle and death are constant," Baldwin tells us in *Fire* that without doubt "so is love."[13]

Even as Baldwin celebrates love's power, he is sharp in his analysis of how human beings resist love's unruly demands for human connection. In *The Amen Corner*, where Baldwin first explicitly explores the character and nature of love, it is the religious institution of the church that most embodies humanity's resistance to love. The first line that Baldwin actually wrote for the play expresses the sense of danger love conveys against those who try to contain its fiery fury. The line was placed on Margaret's tongue in the third act of the play after an argument with her son. She says: "It's a awful thing to think about, the way love never dies." During their argument, the son, David, like the young James Baldwin, shows his determination to leave the care of his family and church to follow his muse into the nightclubs, where sweaty bodies sway in their celebration of the blues. Earlier, before their confrontation, Margaret remembers how intensely she once loved her estranged husband and father of their son. Luke always made her laugh almost enough to let her forget the heartache he could also cause. "Ain't no man never made me laugh the way Luke could," Margaret tells her sister Odessa. She encounters Luke toward the end of the second act and overhears him sharing some thoughts with their son in a room plastered with the music the two men loved. Margaret confesses to Odessa her continued love for Luke despite all the heartache. She tells her sister that because she "bore that man his only son" she will always have some love for him.[14]

When Margaret says of love, "It's a awful thing to think about," she betrays the helplessness she feels before her love for Luke and how she wishes she could contain its fire. But it is at the climax of the play that Baldwin most explicitly pits the workings of love against the rigidities of the institutional church. Only when Margaret leaves the pulpit for perhaps the last time does she reckon with the expansiveness of love that goes far beyond the church as a human institution. With this painful recognition she confesses: "I'm just now finding out what it means to love the Lord. It ain't all in the singing and the shouting. It ain't all in the reading of the Bible." Instead, Margaret suggests that to love God is to love absolutely everyone without reservation and to "suffer with them and rejoice with them and never count the cost."[15]

This expansive love is rooted in the miracle of bodily connection. Early in Baldwin's last novel, *Just Above My Head*, the narrator, Hall Montana, describes his deep love for his wife's body after another joyful bout of sexual activity. For Hall, their coupling demonstrates how sexual intimacy can reveal not only the beauty and wonder of his wife's body, but also the beauty and wonder that abounds in the workings of the everyday. Hall smells her lingering body fragrance on the bed sheets and muses, "Every inch of her body is a miracle for me; maybe because her body has taught me so much about the miracle of my own."[16] Baldwin's vision of love is a bracing one. From the rigors of childbirth to the funk after sex, Baldwin sees our fleshy bodies as the very vehicles of love and grace. For Baldwin, true grace could not come any other way. He is infuriated when religious leaders use the traditional myths at the center of Christian faith—like that of the Virgin Birth—to restrict what can be considered holy. He resents when church leaders and members in his youth set boundaries around the sexual and the profane. But even as Baldwin strives to distance himself from the evangelical heritage he believes would condemn a man like him, Baldwin is still shaped by his parents' religion. This heritage shapes not only Baldwin's sense of identity but also how he understands and conveys the character of love he believes has no bounds.

"An Act of Confession": Sexual Ecstasy and the Nature of Revelatory Experience

Before the wonder of sexual intimacy, Baldwin seems nearly speechless before the revelatory possibilities of fleshy bodies (often of the same sex) coming together in love or at least desire. The mystery that is often associated with divine revelation is what grants gods and human rulers alike the authority and deference to exercise power over human beings. It is this same quality of inexpressible mystery that Baldwin attaches to love. In *Another Country* when he describes Eric's same-sex desires, Baldwin invokes ancient stories and myths as he depicts the frighteningly mysterious and revelatory demands of love. For Baldwin, revelations, whether related to religion or love, are not simply received, they are borne. So when Eric, flush with his newfound love for Yves, remembers a similarly forbidden love for LeRoy, a black boyhood companion, Baldwin's prose bristles with a language often used to describe the terrible, irresistible presence of sacred mystery.

> [T]here was something unspoken between them, something unspeakable, undone, and hideously desired. And yet, of that far-off, burning day, through his knowledge clamored in him and fell all around him, like the sun, and everything in him was aching and yearning for the act, he could not, to save his soul, have named it. It had yet to reach the threshold of his imagination; and it had no name, no name for him anyway, though for other people, so he had heard, it had dreadful names. It had only a shape and the shape was LeRoy and LeRoy contained the mystery which had him by the throat.[17]

When Eric later considers what he learned about himself in this encounter with LeRoy that "had him by the throat," Baldwin's language proceeds with a nearly religious cadence. Similar to a religious conversion experience, Eric's new discovery finds him suddenly confronted by a newly disclosed reality that is as burdensome as it is real. It takes him years "to accept what he, that day, in those arms discovered." Even fifteen year later, when Eric finds himself in the throes of an intensely loving same-sex relationship, he struggles to find a way "to bear that revelation" of long ago. "For the meaning of revelation," Baldwin writes, "must be borne."[18] His sexual experiences have brought Eric a new level of self-awareness with all the anguish that was present at Baldwin's conversion at Mother Horn's church. Sexual expression, it seems from *Another Country*, can disturb and shape one's identity in ways that suggest the religious conversions of old. And so, Baldwin's first experiences of a terrible divine presence that nearly consumed him on the floor of Mother's Horn's church seem to traffic in the same language of the "unspoken" and "unspeakable" that his tabooed desires do.

This connection between the two experiences demonstrates that Baldwin's understanding of the body and sex goes beyond his denunciations of a Christian tradition that engages in sexual repression. His understanding of human creativity and sex as deeply revelatory of the human personality cannot help but be, in part, derived from his evangelical heritage. The very language Baldwin uses to describe sexual intimacy—as an "act of confession"—suggests a deep connection between his understanding of sex and religion. While Baldwin perceives black church culture as a barrier against true sexual expression, his sense of the revelatory, which he drives from his early evangelicalism, still structures his understanding and depiction of how creativity, sexuality, and self-awareness operate and develop together in human community. In a previous chapter I was concerned with how Baldwin used sexual imagery to explore religious practices. Here I am focused on how the language of religion informs how Baldwin describes sex.

Like the many detractors of early revival camp meetings in the nineteenth century who were suspicious of the potential of illicit sexual commingling between men and women and blacks and whites, Baldwin often highlights in his fiction the connections between sexual release and religious ecstasy. By drawing these connections, Baldwin begins to delineate the revelatory and sacramental possibilities of sex. Beyond the suggestive homoerotic language in his earliest novels, Baldwin is much more explicit in making these connections between sex and spiritual revelation in his later work, such as his 1974 *If Beale Street Could Talk*. The intense connection Baldwin makes between the two is demonstrated very early on in the novel when the narrator, Tish, asks her beau, Fonny, during their courtship whether his parents "ever made love together." "Yeah," Fonny answers, "But not like you and me." Then he describes at length how he used to overhear their bedroom activities. His mother, "wet and funky" from her exertions during Sunday morning worship, could only achieve sexual release if she pretended that her sinful husband was Jesus. Even after intense coital activity with her husband, it seemed "[s]he still belonged to Jesus."[19]

Baldwin, of course, goes beyond surface criticism of Christianity's basic confusion about human sexuality. Indeed in *Beale Street* Baldwin does not limit himself to superficial criticism of Fonny's mother and holiness culture's sexual dysfunction, but by invoking religious imagery and themes he also celebrates the physical love Fonny and Tish share. In recounting a memorable bout of lovemaking, Tish hearkens back to how Fonny "rode deeper and deeper not so much into me as into a kingdom which lay just behind his eyes."[20] Literary scholar Trudier Harris builds on Tish's memories to suggest that Baldwin creates "religion of love" that gives the love Tish and Fonny share "a sacred quality" and radically extends and subverts traditional Christian notions for a new and thoroughly secular environment. According to Harris, in *Beale Street* Baldwin attempts "to recapture the essence of Christianity and plant its tenets in new and fertile ground."[21] As Baldwin writes later in the voice of Tish, "When two people love each other, when they really love each other, everything that happens between them has something of a sacramental air."[22]

Even as *Beale Street* demonstrates how central Baldwin's claim about love is for his artistic and moral vision, it also shows just how deeply his religious heritage has shaped his deepest notions of the body and love. Critics have noted how the notion of revelation itself is repeated throughout his novels. But in truth revelation as a concept is crucial in much of his later nonfiction as well.

In "Every Good-Bye Ain't Gone," published in the late 1970s, Baldwin speculates how the notion of revelation actually structures his understanding of life.
"I suspect, though I certainly cannot prove it," Baldwin writes, "that every life
moves full circle—toward revelation: You begin to see, and even rejoice to see,
what you always saw."[23] Baldwin consistently relates revelation to the strangeness and mystery of bodily connection. At the close of *The Devil Finds Work*,
Baldwin writes, "To encounter oneself is to encounter the other: and this is
love. If I know that my soul trembles, I know that yours does, too: and if I can
respect this, both of us can live."[24] Perhaps what distinguishes love from other
revelatory experiences, Baldwin suggests, is that love is contingent on a basic
self-awareness and transparency that the religious variety does not demand.
Baldwin knows his lover's soul trembles precisely because he accepts that his
own soul trembles as well.

But even as Baldwin continues to suggest how important the character of
revelatory experience is to understanding life and love, he subverts our expectations of how the revelatory should actually work in human lives for the better.
Of course, for Baldwin, revelation, whether sacred or profane, shapes the bodies and behaviors of those under its sway just as Eric's sexual desires in *Another
Country* are "inscribed in every one of his gestures" and "betrayed in every
inflection of his voice."[25] Critics, however, generally miss how ambiguous any
revelation can be for Baldwin. As Kevin Ohi in a recent article on *Another Country* argues, "Critics fail to note that self-revelation almost always appears in the
novel as poignantly yearned-for impossibility. Revelation appears only in the
guise of its failure."[26] Where some critics note Baldwin's continual invocation of
revelation in his writings in an effort to suggest a religious meaning behind his
work, they have not come to terms with the fundamental ambiguity that informs
and shapes Baldwin's reflection on it in his novels and nonfiction.[27] Surprisingly,
Baldwin often characterizes the sexually revelatory as a moment filled with
anguish even for those in pursuit of authentic and unrepressed sexual expression. While he accepts the sacred dimensions of love, Baldwin, the very apostle
of bodily love, seems captive to a perspective that considers the coupling of
human bodies to be a principal source for profound alienation as well.

When Ida and Vivaldo fall feverishly into bed together and begin a tumultuous interracial love affair in *Another Country*, Baldwin describes the aftermath
that punctuates an evening of desire and begins a relationship filled with strain
and difficulty. As Vivaldo looks into the darker hued countenance of his new
lover, he sees a face "more mysterious and impenetrable than the face of any
stranger." In this poignant description of sexual discovery, the face of a new
lover, Baldwin suggests, is not only "unknown" and but also "a mystery, con-
taining, *like all mysteries, the possibility of torment.*"[28] Even as Baldwin celebrates

the importance of bodily love, he often suggests, as he does here, that some desperate sexual unions can bring more mystery and alienation than self-awareness. Or perhaps, to the extent any human relationships, desperate or not, can be called revelatory, what they in fact reveal is the torment and alienation that underlies all human experience. Even when Tish in *Beale Street* describes her first joyous coupling of what will be an immensely fruitful relationship filled with promise and hope, she laces her language with hints of the strangeness and the sense of alienation that defines all human relationships. At that moment Tish says: "It's astounding the first time you realize that a stranger has a body—the realization that he has a body makes him a stranger. It means that you have a body, too. You will live with this forever, and it will spell out the language of your life."[29]

Some contemporary literary scholars, particularly those influenced by gay and lesbian critical theorists, might suggest that these moments of ambiguity only demonstrate the extent to which Baldwin was trapped in the partially closeted existence that characterized much of gay life before the modern gay liberation movement. As critic William Cohen writes, "It is now clear just how closeted the pre-Stonewall setting of Baldwin's novel [*Another Country*] is: There is no coming out the closet because there is nowhere to come out to. Sexuality was, there, 'perfectly' private—it had not yet found a public voice."[30] Baldwin certainly gives some credence to this reading in his interview with Richard Goldstein in 1984. During the exchange, Baldwin confesses that the word *gay* had "always rubbed me the wrong way." When Goldstein continues to press Baldwin on whether he ever thought of himself as gay, Baldwin responds: "[W]hen I began to realize things about myself, began to suspect who I was and what I was likely to become, it was still very *personal, absolutely personal*. It was really a matter between me and God."[31]

Assuredly, Baldwin's connection to the modern gay and lesbian liberation movement is a complicated one. In this same interview, it is clear that Baldwin associates many aspects of the modern gay rights movement with white privilege.[32] But there is also little doubt that Baldwin comes to consciousness long before the Stonewall rebellion, which along with many other events and examples of broad-based activism throughout the United States, signaled for many gays and lesbians a new unwillingness to stay in the closet. Stonewall announced a bolder engagement with sexuality and a demand that a homophobic society create room in the public square for what was once deemed private. So to some extent Cohen and others are right to criticize Baldwin's vision as harboring a cramped notion of freedom. In light of the devastation of AIDS, Baldwin's pronouncements that he was actually freer because he eschewed labels others adopted would now clearly be a masquerade. But perhaps

Baldwin's ambivalence suggests something else. Perhaps it suggests how ingrained Christianity's rejection of the body truly is in black religion. For an enslaved people, a perspective that denies bodily reality certainly could be seen as more attractive than many contemporary scholars of black religion would like to admit. And even Baldwin, who had come largely to reject this vision of black evangelicalism and who celebrated the body more than any other major black cultural figure with the exception of Audre Lorde, could not shake off the possibility of a sudden revelation from without—from beyond the self and the ordinary cosmos. It is only as Baldwin sketches out the very limits of god-talk that he truly begins to subvert and move beyond the conversion- and revelation-brokered religion of his ancestors.

White Supremacy as a Threat to Black Manhood

Shortly after his traumatic conversion, Baldwin became a traveling minister active throughout Harlem. Baldwin's life as a popular boy minister in Harlem most assuredly shaped his portrayal of Julia, who also spends much of her early life as a "fire-baptized child evangelist" in *Just Above My Head*. Julia mirrors Baldwin's own sentiments toward the church when she, early in the novel, recalls her feelings right before giving a eulogy for Mother Bessie Green: "And then, I thought—for the first time that maybe that was why I'd entered the pulpit in the first place. Because I was so far from God in my own house, so far from anyone who loved me. The love of God was the first love I knew anything about. I *will* say: it brought me from a long ways off."[33]

For Baldwin, the limitations of the evangelical Christianity of his youth are stark and real. Even so, Baldwin acknowledges that what he knows about love and its importance is derived in part from his exposure to the beliefs and practices of various churches. Clearly, as he became more involved as a minister, Baldwin gained a measure of autonomy from his highly restrictive father, which he relished. Preaching at least once a week, the young Baldwin drew larger crowds as he gained preaching prowess beyond the talents of his father. And Baldwin admits in *Fire* that he "ruthlessly" pressed the advantage his popularity gave him over his father. The church was the first context where Baldwin found power as he achieved his manhood and love. For this "frog-eyed" boy it was also the first place where he felt the paternal love he craved, even if it was only from an imaginary god.[34]

But the love at the core of the church's message was undermined and subverted, in Baldwin's eyes, with the church's focus on revenge and judgment. Baldwin demonstrates this in his last published work, *The Evidence of Things Not Seen*. At the close of this essay, Baldwin remembers how Buddy, a young teenage boy from his church "backslid," or lost his commitment for the rigors of the religious community. So when Buddy died of tuberculosis before reaching adulthood, Baldwin and his then-religious community believed that he had died "in sin" and presumably was on his way to hell. Where Baldwin once accepted this proposition, looking back he rejects the exclusion of supposed infidels from the universal reign of God. Noting the words of Jesus, who according to the Fourth Gospel refused the demands of religious leaders who wanted to condemn a prostitute to death, Baldwin now regrets that he joined his church community in condemning Buddy. As Baldwin writes, "*Let him who is without sin among you cast the first stone.* But I could not say that, then. It was when I found myself unable *not* to say it that I, too, left the church — the community; and it took me many years to realize that the community that had formed me had also brought about that hour and that rupture."[35]

In their refusal to accept everyone, black churches like their white counterparts expose the narrow parochialism at the heart of traditional Christianity. Baldwin would in fact ask in *Fire* whether heaven was "merely another ghetto." With this question, Baldwin challenges black churches' insularity and their uneasy relationship with the demands and broad universal reach of love. Because of this insularity, Baldwin asserts that in fact there is "no love in the church." What the church offered instead with its vengeful god and its neat and absolute distinctions between heaven and hell — saints and sinners — was really "a mask for hatred and self-hatred and despair."[36] By not living up to the values and standards of its founder, the church is guilty not simply of hypocrisy but also of barely disguised hatred of life in all its forms, particularly as expressed in people's desire for sexual fulfillment. What he termed "the sexual paranoia of the United States" includes and goes beyond homophobia to a kind of "life-phobia" and is demonstrated in the number of young people who, in Baldwin's words, would sooner go "on the needle" rather than admit "they might want to go to bed with someone of the same sex."[37]

While his analysis on America's sexual paranoia is broad and extends to include the difficulties of those who share same-sex love, Baldwin's own focus on sexuality and the body begins with the black experience of slavery in the United States. "The sexual question and the racial question," Baldwin tells Richard Goldstein in an interview, "have always been entwined."[38] For Baldwin, Americans' denial of sex and the body originate with the slave auction block. Clearly remembering how white men (and women) sexually exploited him, Baldwin tells biographer Fern Eckman, "If you're a Negro, you're the center of the *peculiar* affliction because *anybody* can touch *you* . . . [and] you're the target for everybody's fantasies." Black women, Baldwin continues, were forced to do things that a white man "wouldn't ask his wife to do."[39] "In this country," Baldwin tells Studs Terkel, "the Negro pays for that guilt which white people have about the flesh."[40] In an early review of a Chester Himes's book, Baldwin is even more explicit, revealing his own latent sexism when he explodes: "One might over-simplify our racial heritage sufficiently to observe . . . that its essentials would seem to be contained in the tableau of a black and white man facing and that the root of our trouble is between their legs."[41]

Baldwin's intense exploration of sex and race is seen most clearly as he grapples throughout his work with the hypereroticized black male body in much of American culture. In his short story "Going to Meet the Man," for example, Baldwin in the course of his portrayal of a white lawman describes what he believes to be the pathology of white male sexuality. The protagonist is a white sheriff who is depicted, in the words of one Baldwin biographer, as "tragically imprisoned in the myth of black sexuality that dominates his psychic world."[42] The inspiration for this short story came from an encounter Baldwin had during his southern tour during the late 1950s. In his *No Name in the Street,* written nearly fifteen years later, Baldwin writes about his "unbelieving shock" when he realized that he "was being groped by one of the most powerful men in one of the states I visited." Baldwin sees this sexual assault through the lenses of his history. Drunk with "his wet eyes staring" in Baldwin's face and "his wet hands grouping" for his penis, this man had them "both, abruptly, in history's ass-pocket." In describing the effects and implications of this assault, Baldwin continues: "It was very frightening—not the gesture itself, but the abjectness of it, and the assumption of a swift and grim complicity: as my identity was defined by his power, so was my humanity to be placed at the service of his fantasies." Baldwin then understood that this official, given his position and the assurance whiteness brings, could have Baldwin lynched even though he was the one who had initiated the sexual intrusion. As Baldwin reckoned with the reality of his own powerlessness, he knew that he still had to remain friendly. But there was a price. And "the price," Baldwin writes, was his "cock"—that is, his bodily integrity and dignity as a man.[43]

For Baldwin, the legacy of slavery is most simply expressed as this loss of black manhood. This legacy is what informs Baldwin's perception of history's "ass-pocket" in 1957. Baldwin tapped into these racial and sexual currents in the culture in one of his first published stories. In "Previous Condition," published in 1948, Baldwin writes a scene in which a white landlady evicts Peter, a young black New York City actor. Only after she discovers his race does the landlady demand his eviction. "I can't have no colored people here," she says. "All my tenants are complainin'. Women afraid to come home nights."[44] In an unpublished manuscript, Baldwin, in a section that would be partially excised from the published version, refers more directly to the sexual myths associated with black men than his editors at *Commentary* magazine felt comfortable with. In the original version, Peter taunts his landlady with lightly charged sexual innuendo. In his imagination, he gives a response to her demands that he does not dare give in reality. "I almost said," Baldwin writes in Peter's voice, "Let's go to bed together, you maggot-eaten bitch, because I knew that in the back of her mind she was recalling every rape story she had ever heard, every dirty darky story ever told."[45]

These ruminations on how sexual myths surrounding black men shaped the dreams and fantasies of white men and women were not idle speculation. For Baldwin, they were based on actual encounters he had with white men and women during his early twenties in Greenwich Village during a period when he was most intensely confronting and exploring his own sexuality. Baldwin complains in one essay about how many women wanted to "civilize" him and how many men wanted him to act out "the role of darky" in their sexual play. He bemoans how often whites fixated during their sexual encounters on "speculations concerning the size of his [sexual] organ."[46] Toward the end of his life, Baldwin became more and more graphic in engaging these issues. The stakes were high and Baldwin now refused to sugarcoat what he perceived were the multitudinous threats to black manhood. "Every black man walking in this country pays a tremendous price for walking," Baldwin writes, "for men are not women, and a man's balance depends on the weight he carries between his legs." Referring even to the biblical legends of creation, Baldwin continues: "All men . . . know something about each other, which is simply that a man without balls is not a man; the word *genesis* describes the male, involves the phallus, and refers to the seed which gives life. When one man can no longer honor this in another man . . . he has abdicated from a man's estate, and hard upon the heels of that abdication, chaos arrives."[47]

With his celebration of the male's capacity for creation and reproduction, Baldwin erases women's central place in reproduction and replaces it with an all-too-familiar fixation on male prowess. Given his willingness to obscure the central place women hold in creation, it is perhaps not surprising that Baldwin sometimes seems so blind to the crucial question of sexism in his analysis of white supremacy. This blindness is highlighted in Baldwin's answer to a question a white woman posed at the end of his lecture at DePaul University in 1986, near the end of his life. When asked whether his analysis of racial oppression could be expanded to include women, "Baldwin flatly responded that white women were not oppressed. And black women to the degree that they were oppressed, suffered the oppression of race."[48] Although Baldwin occasionally discussed the brutal use of black women's bodies by white slaveholders and their descendants, he generally did not confront the brutality many black women faced from their black male companions.

It is ironic that despite Baldwin's longtime focus on the importance of black manhood that many black nationalists, no doubt motivated by their own homophobia, would condemn Baldwin throughout the late 1960s and the early 1970s as a sellout and an "Uncle Tom," and suggest that his expression of a gay sexuality was a sign both of his weakness and of his co-optation by white political and cultural elites.[49] After these attacks, Baldwin makes clear that for him the prime effect of white supremacy was the loss of black manhood. Perhaps it was defensive of Baldwin, who in *No Name in the Street* declares white supremacy as most directly a problem of the black phallus. He continues again and again in this essay to depict the problems and effects of white supremacy around the rights of the black patriarch to the exclusion of other members of the black community. As Baldwin would emphasize: "the black man's right to his women, as well as to his children, was simply taken from him."[50]

Sex, Love, and the Limits of God

In any case, the West's erotic fixation on the black body that Baldwin ably describes not only reveals the crucial psychosexual dimensions of white supremacy but also reveals the limits of the traditional notion of God. Baldwin suggests that for many white Christians, God had become "a metaphor for purity and for safety" that paradoxically allowed a self-destructive lack of awareness about the absolute demands of love and the reality of suffering.[51] As Baldwin told one interviewer in 1984, "Loving anybody and being loved by anybody is a tremendous danger, a tremendous responsibility."[52] So perched within a God-given "purity" and what Baldwin calls "a very biblical culture," Western Christians become free to avoid the terrible responsibilities of true love when they engage in self-repression in their attempt to escape the terror the fear of death can bring.[53] In his speech before the WCC in 1968, Baldwin linked the self-repression that denies the value of sexual intimacy associated with Saint Paul, the early desert fathers, and Augustine with how the black body has been denigrated in Western culture generally. "There is a sense in which it can be said," Baldwin told the crowd, "that my black flesh is the flesh that Saint Paul wanted to have mortified." Baldwin believes the act of self-repression at the center of Christian views of the body that Paul initiated has split "the Christian personality" in two, leaving itself "bewildered" and "at war with itself." Just as Baldwin denounces white supremacy, he asserts that in truth the flesh and spirit are indivisible and that the split within the Christian personality that supports white supremacy must be overcome. As Baldwin told the international community of Christians in Sweden: "From my point of view, it seems to me the flesh and the spirit are one; it seems to me that when you mortify the one, you have mortified the other."[54]

This split in the Christian personality has created a legacy that has contributed to a profound inability to confront real suffering and the artistic expressions that emerge from pain. Baldwin in that same speech accused Westerners of being "unable to comprehend the force of such a woman as Mahalia Jackson . . . [and] unable to accept the depth of sorrow, out of which a Ray Charles comes." He suggests that before the blues rhythms that underlie the work of Mahalia Jackson and Ray Charles many white people were befuddled at the depths of suffering and the art and music it gives rise to even as they inform and shape the black struggle for identity and freedom. Before this embodied expression of pain and suffering, European heirs to Christianity were caught in a form of mass schizophrenia that leaves especially those in this nation disfigured by their inability to apprehend the tragic in life. It remains an open question whether anything can be retained from the traditional Christian notions of a personal external god, but for Baldwin the attempt to carve a progressive vision from his black evangelical heritage required him to jostle God to the sidelines. Even though the silent presence (or absence) of God haunts all of his work, Baldwin struggles to keep at the center of his moral vision the blues, rather than god-talk, as the embodied expression that emerges from the depths of black suffering.

Like many existentialist thinkers, Baldwin, as he considers the nature of human life, begins with a conception of the cosmos that assumes its indifference to the suffering and striving of human beings for identity and purpose, and rejects the notion of God or natural law. In one early essay, "The Preservation of Innocence," published in 1949, Baldwin deeply ponders how the notion of "nature" has been used to exclude the reality of same-sex desire and intimacy. "[W]henever nature is invoked to support our human divisions," Baldwin warns, we have "every right to be suspicious." Later, Baldwin notes how human beings, in fact, have long resisted and resented nature's power over human aspirations, partly because nature had no discernible concern for human beings or their institutions. It is in his assessment of the possibilities of our collective human will to assert meaning and purpose before the "implacable power" of nature that Baldwin begins a description of the origins of the sacred in the human imagination:

> I suspect, that he [God] sprang into being on the cold, black day when we discovered that nature cared nothing for us. His advent, which alone had the power to save us from nature and ourselves, also created self-awareness . . . . It marked the death of innocence; it set up the duality of good-and-evil . . . . [T]he homosexual did not exist; nor properly speaking did the heterosexual. We are all in a state of nature.

Without nature's validation, and in the course of struggle and suffering, human communities imagine a god—an imaginary entity Baldwin calls "man's most intense creation"—who rushes forward to establish rigid rules, labels, and

categories such as homosexuality and heterosexuality to comfort those frightened at the sheer messiness and complicity of life.[55]

Recognizing his own capacity for the joy of same-sex desire and expression,
Baldwin goes beyond his characterization of the sacred in *Go Tell It*. There, the
divine is depicted as an illusionary refuge built by a human desire for safety
even as it is undone by the grittiness of an urban secular life filled with artistic
and sexual possibilities. In "Preservation of Innocence," Baldwin fleshes out
more explicitly than in his first novel his indictment of the various constraints
on sexual expression in black religious culture. His tone, with its harsher depiction of the limitations and repression of church mores is in fact strikingly similar in tone to *The Amen Corner*. Pressed against the rigidities of traditional sexual
morality, Baldwin sees this Christian god not only as a human-created illusion
who supplies refuge from a hostile world but also as a tyrant. This autocratic
ruler in the heavens is born in human beings' fear of death, which becomes a
symbol of their capacity for self-loathing as it first labels various kinds of sexual intimacy and then damns them. "[I]t is not in the sight of nature that the
homosexual is condemned," Baldwin writes, "but in the sight of God." But, as
Baldwin also affirms, "human beings . . . cannot ever be labeled."[56]

To the dismay of some contemporary gay theorists, Baldwin himself was
resistant to any attempt to categorize his own sexual behavior as gay, bisexual,
or anything else. For him the central issue was life itself. While Baldwin seriously questioned the existence of God, for him it was his status as a sexual outcast that demonstrates in concrete terms the failure of Christian theism.
Baldwin argued that the Christian god's condemnation of same-sex desire was
a "profound and dangerous failure of concept" because it condemned "an incal-
culable number of the world's humans" to "something less than life."[57] In an
early biography, Baldwin described how these divine injunctions resulted in
this terrible fate: "I know a lot of people who turn into junkies because they're
afraid they might be *queer*."[58] But Baldwin's cries about a malevolent god were
not simply abstract ranting; they were personal. He knew firsthand how these
divine injunctions were contrary to life. When Baldwin embraces the term *life-
phobia* he understands that this deep fear of life is most concretely the fear of
touch. Noting the bias about same-sex desire, Baldwin tells Eckman: "[I]t's not
a fear of men going to bed with men. It's a fear of anybody touching anybody!"
In short, Baldwin delights that "people were born to *touch* each other."[59]

Late in his life while he was teaching at Bowling Green University, an English professor excitedly told Baldwin about a class he was teaching on *Giovanni's
Room* and "the whole question of homosexuality." Ernest Champion, a fellow
teacher at Bowling Green, recorded Baldwin's response: "Baldwin with a very
puzzled look on his face, very innocently asked him, 'Did you say "homosexuality"? But the book is not about homosexuality.' When the professor asked

him what it was about, Baldwin very softly answered, 'It's about love,' turned on his heel and walked away."[60] Where others were determined to fix a label on Baldwin's sexuality and his work, Baldwin resisted. For him, his art and life were all about the decisive importance of physical affection and love in human life. In a 1984 interview with Richard Goldstein, Baldwin repeated what he said in Bowling Green about love and *Giovanni's Room,* but he also confessed that if he had not written this book when he did, "I would probably have had to stop writing altogether." Throughout his conversation with Goldstein, Baldwin demonstrated just how central love and physical intimacy were to his moral and artistic vision. As Baldwin told Goldstein: "The question of human affection, of integrity, in my case, the question of trying to become a writer, are all linked with the question of sexuality. Sexuality is only a part of it. I don't know even if it's the most important part. But it's indispensable."[61] And it was this strong commitment to a love that shatters all boundaries, including those that separate blacks from white, that made Baldwin so uncomfortable with black evangelicals calling implicitly for divine vengeance against whites.

But even as the music and beat of the church shaped his understanding of love and life's vibrant potential, Baldwin continued to invoke the rhetoric of judgment despite all his protests to the contrary. Baldwin understood that an uncontrollable paranoia birthed in the midst of the denial and avoidance of sex and love in American life takes bodily form in the threatening presence of black people who confront many white people with the possibility of their undoing. As Baldwin explores how black people reside as frightful phantoms in the white imagination, he closely equates the "sexual despair" of many whites with the inability to give and receive true love. These loveless white people Baldwin writes about live, in his view, "in a state of carefully repressed terror in relation to blacks." They are haunted as they deny their kinship to the descendents of those their ancestors enslaved and raped. Baldwin believes that the entire nation is in fact "predicated on this denial, this monstrous and pathetic lie."[62]

But by the 1970s, with its social turmoil, Baldwin believed that this lie was now in danger of completely unraveling as those caught up in the lie were making a play toward a false innocence. They were trying to ward off a possible comeuppance in a way that would distort their personality as they placed their very selves in the service of lies and deception. As Baldwin writes again in *No Name:* "It is not true that people become liars without knowing it. A liar always knows he is lying, and that is why liars travel in packs in order to be reassured that the judgment day will never come for them."[63] Remembering his first trip on assignment to the South in 1957 at the very beginning of the modern civil rights movement, Baldwin recalls how his presence by the "white" entrance of a segregated restaurant in Montgomery, Alabama, revealed the repressed "absolute" terror of many white people always lurking beneath the surface.

"Every white face turned to stone," Baldwin recalls, as "the arrival of the messenger of death could not have had a more devastating effect than the appearance in the restaurant doorway of a small, unarmed utterly astounded black man." Suddenly conscious of his northern accent, Baldwin reversed himself and went through the back entrance to sit on a stool in the "colored" section, where he quietly realized that his new writing assignment was going to be "one hell of a gig."[64]

As the tumultuous 1960s slid into the decadent and gradually depoliticized 1970s, Baldwin's celebrity and literary efforts continued to provide him a pulpit to address loveless people clinging to their white identities who often professed an innocence that would prove to be false. During this period, Baldwin still had a firm (though fading) confidence in the expansive and sacramental character and power of love. It was the only thing that could ward off the ultimate destruction of Western civilization. At the conclusion of his famous *Fire* essay, Baldwin urges "the relatively conscious whites and the relatively conscious blacks" to work "like lovers" as they attempt to shape the consciousness of those less aware of the ultimate stakes.[65] But with the publication of *Fire* and the climatic moments of the modern civil rights movement, even while he celebrates how love can create the new consciousness needed for survival, this apostle of love and carnal pleasures from *Giovanni's Room* and *Another Country* also becomes the messenger of death. And this time, with the attention of the national media fixed on him for much of the decade, Baldwin refused to go through the back entrance.

Chapter 5

A Pulpit beyond the Church

activism, fire, and the coming
judgment on (white) america

I hazard that the King James Bible, the rhetoric of the store-front church, something ironic and violent and perpetually understated in Negro speech—and something of Dickens' love for bravura—have something to do with me today.

NOTES OF A NATIVE SON, *1955*

*C*harles Bell, born around 1781 and enslaved for four decades in Maryland, South Carolina, and Georgia, remembered in his popular memoir how fellow slaves burdened with the "evil that has been endured in this life . . . console[d] themselves with the delights of a future state." But these Africans, newly exposed to Christian cosmology, did not simply reflect on how good heaven would be for them; they also relished how bad hell would be for their enslavers. They believed, in short, "that those who tormented them here, will most surely be tormented in their turn hereafter." As Bell wrote,

> It is impossible to reconcile the mind of the native slave to the idea of living in a state of perfect equality, and boundless affection with white people. Heaven will be no heaven to him, if he is not to be avenged of his enemies. I know, from experience, that these are the fundamental rules of his religious creed; because I learned them in the religious meetings of the slaves themselves.[1]

For these enslaved Africans any future heaven that might exist could not be paradise with the presence of their enslavers. Bell finds that this insatiable desire for divine justice and retribution was in fact "a cornerstone" of a still emerging black religious sensibility that coincides in general terms at least with much of the Christian scriptures. "[F]or in that book [the Bible]," Ball reports,

"I find in every where laid down, that those who have possessed an inordinate portion of the good things of this world . . . at the expense of their fellow men will surely have to render an account of their stewardship, and be punished."[2]

Despite these reported parallels between Scripture and the new and still-forming religious ethos of enslaved Africans, these conceptions of hell did not initially emerge just from biblical texts that speak of fire and brimstone; they also sprang naturally from lives lived in bondage—a fully realized hell on earth. May, a former enslaved woman beaten across the head with "tongs" or a "poker" by her slaveholding mistress, remembered in one interview during the late 1920s the brutality of an old male slaveholder in the plantation next to the one she lived on. For May and others of her number, evil was not an amorphous abstraction. Wickedness, instead, had a distinctly personal face. May's slaveholder—a man simply described as "a devil on earth"—kicked several pregnant women and precipitated numerous miscarriages even as he took time to beat women working in the fields who attempted to nurse their hungry children without his permission. May once saw the slaveholder "walk through the field and, seeing a baby crying, take his stick and knock its brains out and call for the foreman to come and haul off the nasty black rat." This murderous reality shaped May's thinking about hell and divine judgment. As she tells the interviewer: "[I]n them days it was hell without fires. This is one reason why I believe in a hell. I don't believe a just God is going to take no such man as that [slaveholder] into his kingdom."[3]

Unlike May, Henry "Box" Brown, another escaped slave, focused divine wrath not simply on the most brutal slaveholder but potentially on all of them. "I believe in a hell, where the wicked will forever dwell and knowing the character of slaveholders and slavery, it is my settled belief," Brown writes, "that *every* slaveholder will infallibly go to that hell, unless he repents."[4] This radical legacy within black Christian thought (with its focus on future divine retribution on the perpetrators and beneficiaries of slavery) was passed on to Baldwin and his generation from their parents and grandparents born in slavery. Although many black people retreated in the face of the racial terror of the post-Reconstruction period, throughout the South and the rest of the country, a coded, religious language that reflected a keen desire for justice and retribution remained a central feature in much of Afro-Protestantism. This emphasis caused no small measure of consternation for the young Baldwin as he achieved his adulthood and shaped his initial destiny outside the institutional confines of the church.

Baldwin's problems with Christianity, of course, began with his refusal to withdraw from the world and its physical pleasures of art, drink, and sex. For Baldwin, the deep desire for a safe refuge from the world animates a religious devotion that restricts human potential and hampers an open embrace of life despite its dangers. Baldwin's initial withdrawal from black holiness culture and the institutional confines of the church hardened into a principled rejection of Christianity in the face of the seemingly permanent character of black suffering. Baldwin's rejection only solidified as he saw how a narrow parochialism could dominate the Christian faith of his youth, despite all its pretensions to having a generous universal spirit. Just as Baldwin saw the limits of God — or, at least, the limits of Christian god-talk — he also keenly felt the limits in the language of revenge and vengeance that he felt characterized much of black religion.

Like Charles Ball, Baldwin knew that judgment rhetoric was intrinsic to many aspects of black religious expression. Various black religious groups from the early evangelicals of the nineteenth century to the contemporary religious nationalism of the Nation of Islam have all invoked and asserted the coming reality of a divine judgment that would punish a wayward nation for its sins against African people. For many black people, religion in Baldwin's words would seem to operate "as a complete and exquisite fantasy revenge" where white people are punished and (righteous) black people rewarded. These religious persons on the underside of Western imperialism and chattel slavery could only hope that this dramatic reversal would happen soon. In Baldwin's words, they hope that indeed "God is not sleeping" and that "the judgment is not far off."[5] Within this desire for retribution, a black evangelical rhetoric that embraces a cosmology with a hell can be understood as coded language that cloaks its hostility toward a white elite. In this strife-ridden world, "bitterness," Baldwin adds wryly, "is neither dead or sleeping," even if God is. From this perspective, judgment rhetoric becomes a kind of "hidden transcript" — often misread by outsiders — that in fact suggests a deeper culture of resistance toward the dominant society.[6]

As Baldwin reckons with this heritage, he often pretends to be scandalized by the anger and thirst for vengeance that hover just beneath the surface of the pious posturing that often marks black religion. But even as Baldwin pronounces how he has rejected the "apocalypse" that was "central" to his father's vision, he continues to invoke its themes and its rhetoric throughout his work. As Baldwin himself acknowledges in the epigraph to this chapter: "I hazard that the King James Bible, the rhetoric of the store-front church, something *ironic and violent* and perpetually understated in Negro speech — and something of Dickens' love for bravura — have something to do with me today."[7] So despite his avowed distaste for the harsh rhetoric of vengeance, Baldwin retained some of the "irony and violence" common to the language that animated black culture in his youth. With his bestseller, *The Fire Next Time,*

Baldwin harnessed the "perpetually understated" character of coded evangelical speech to persuade a much wider audience that the cause for human and civil rights during the 1960s was a just cause.

Perhaps because he had distanced himself from the vengeful themes of judgment, Baldwin's initial use of this rhetoric in the second essay of *Fire* had a slightly impersonal quality. In this work, the Christian god is shorn of personality and is described and understood as a cold force that structures the moral arc of the universe just like the Newtonian natural laws were found, with the emergence of the Enlightenment and the scientific method, to shape the physical world. The picture of an impersonal, faceless deity replaces the personal and vengeful one of Baldwin's youth. This transformation is signaled most directly at the end of *Fire* with a sharp warning from Baldwin to those white Americans reluctant to grant full citizenship to the progeny of enslaved Africans. In *Fire* Baldwin worries that a mixture of "intransigence" and "ignorance" in white America might make a kind of cosmic "vengeance inevitable" where the very viability of American society is challenged. This cosmic vengeance is not "executed by," as Baldwin explains it, "*any person or organization,*" but instead works inexorably like gravity and comes "based on the law that we recognize when we say, 'Whatever goes up must come down.'"[8]

Despite Baldwin's mechanistic language, the influence of the biblical myths that shaped his early life is still clear. But Baldwin's turn toward the faceless deity of natural law signals just how much he is willing to divest himself of the adornment that often comes with religious rhetoric. Baldwin does more, however, than simply constrain the cadences of King James English, whose very rhythms suggest a universe filled with sacred majesty. He also tries throughout his work to translate the divine reality of old into an intensely realized humanism where God no longer retains a place outside of creation but in fact is acknowledged as "an act of creation on the part of every human being."[9] Of course, Baldwin's continued invocation of a revelation that still seems to come beyond the self, suggests that his efforts were not entirely successful. Even so, for Baldwin, God largely becomes an outgrowth of humanity's own collective creative powers. In this world, divine injunctions, emptied of past references to supernatural occurrences from beyond human history, become, instead, expressions of collective human creativity and imagination. It is from this context that Baldwin begins to modify his long-standing and often foreboding sense of divine malevolence. As he describes a universe uncaring to the interests of black life, he tries to discount any connection he might have had to the frightfully capricious deity of biblical mythology. Instead of complaining about a deity callous to human suffering and seated emperor-like in the heavens as divine judgments are meted out against a sinful humankind, Baldwin inveighs in less personal terms against this universe that "has evolved no terms" for the existence of black people.[10] Again, Baldwin's success is mixed. Pushed by a sense of cosmic injustice, he continues, despite himself, to struggle against a god he does not fully (if at all) believe in.

But despite this partial demotion of God from a vibrant personality to a joy-less force of nature, Baldwin's language crackles with the heat of moral indig-nation and promises of a surely coming doom. His language passes judgment on the United States even as it reveals the inadequacies of American society. As Baldwin writes:

> Time catches up with kingdoms and crushes them, gets its teeth into doc-trines and rends them; time reveals the foundations on which any kingdom rests and eats at those foundations, and it destroys doctrines by proving them to be untrue. In those days, not so very long ago, when the priests of that church which stands in Rome gave God's blessing to Italian boys being sent out to ravage a defenseless black country—which until that event, incidentally had not considered itself to be black—it was not pos-sible to believe in a black God. To entertain such a belief would have been to entertain madness. But time has passed, and in that time the Christian world has revealed itself as morally bankrupt and politically unstable.[11]

Baldwin, once again, renders judgment on American society not through the invocation of a brooding Christian god but through the blind inexorability of history. He warns that the white Christian god will be discredited and "crushed" in time and that new (black) gods will arise in the future. But despite the impersonal quality of language, Baldwin's judgment rhetoric gains a more personal edge over time. This emerging perspective in fact marries Baldwin's criticisms of institutional Christianity with his suspicions about the nature of white pathology and its destructive role in world culture. Together, these inter-rogations of Christianity and white identity provide a platform for Baldwin's critique of Western culture as a whole. Baldwin fears that the cancer he describes as at the center of the white social identity will be the final trigger for the collapse of an imperial—yet "morally bankrupt"—Western society. To avoid this ultimate catastrophe, Baldwin urges that "everything white Ameri-cans think they believe" must "be reexamined." The consequences of not con-ducting this self-inventory are for Baldwin too horrible to contemplate. As Baldwin concludes in *Fire:* "If we do not now dare everything, the fulfillment of that prophecy, recreated from the Bible in song by a slave is upon us: *God gave Noah the rainbow sign, No more water, the fire next time!*"[12]

But following the publication of *Fire* in early 1963, Baldwin became more exasperated with many white liberals and what he perceived as their failure to

reject privilege based on white social identity. He quickly tires of the false innocence many of his old liberal friends clung to when they were confronted
directly with the effects of this privilege. Baldwin marveled at the extent to
which many white people denied any real kinship of blood and circumstance
with their black compatriots. As his patience with white liberals ebbed, Baldwin
lost any hope of divesting himself of the irony and violence intrinsic to the
judgment rhetoric of the black evangelicalism of his youth. For Baldwin, the
ancient language of hell became the point of departure for a broad exploration
into the nature of white privilege in America. For Baldwin this "revenge fantasy" at the core of black religion was tied up with how many black people
linked the white privilege they witnessed everyday with the ongoing hell of their
lives since slavery. Baldwin in *Fire* remembers how a minister from the Nation
of Islam captured this insight, singing, "The white man's Heaven . . . is the black
man's Hell." And although Baldwin concedes that this phrase "puts the matter
somewhat too simply," he also claims "it has been true for as long as white men
have ruled the world."[13] So although Baldwin initially casts his "violent and
ironic" language in heated but almost mechanistic terms, during the 1960s and
1970s his language increasingly targets, with growing emotional and personal
force, the hallow hubris and ignorance at the core of white social identity.

With this increasingly pointed message, Baldwin exchanged the private
local pulpit of his youth for the public one his celebrity provided. In an essay
written in the 1980s, Baldwin bemoans his native country's tendency for "self-
congratulation": "If I were still in the pulpit which some people (and they may
be right) claim I never left, I would counsel my countrymen to the self-con-
frontation of prayer, the cleansing breaking of the heart which precedes atonement."[14] With this statement he not only reprises the language of the church
but also confesses his long-standing role as a preacher and moralist. Baldwin's
unique voice would combine a language that preached love's power with a perspective that deconstructed the very notion of whiteness. The first impulse con-
verged with the dominant organizing principle of a cresting black freedom
movement that relied on an integrationist ethic. The second ran in the path of
a well-worn apocalyptic sensibility and served along with the iconic example of
Malcolm X as a wellspring for an emergent modern black nationalism in
SNCC and the Black Panther Party of the late 1960s and early 1970s. His
voice was popular for a time because it successfully wed urgent appeals to the
morality of white liberals with a harsh honest scolding that pricked their guilty
consciences. But his voice was most notable as a bridge between two strains
within black culture. His middle position became increasingly marginal, however, as a rising nationalist perspective challenged the reigning civil rights coali-
tion and many white elites and progressives weary of the ever-more pressing

calls for racial justice turned to other business like protesting the war in Vietnam. But the power of Baldwin's speech always depended on his poetic connection with black religion and his intimate conversations with and connections to white power.

Conversations with Power: The Destructiveness of Willful Innocence

Aching for a drink, Baldwin could still feel the heat from his charged confrontation with the attorney general of the United States. He was seated and preparing for his interview in a hot television studio in New York City with Kenneth Clark, who was at that time the most prominent and influential black psychologist in the United States. Clark and Baldwin had traveled together in a cab after a failed meeting with Robert Kennedy that had been hurriedly arranged in the wake of the upheaval at Birmingham. With the historic clash between civil rights activists and the fire hoses of the thuggish sheriff Bull Conner broadcast across the nation's television, Baldwin had sent an outraged telegram to Kennedy in mid-May of 1963. Aided by his sudden celebrity with the publication of *Fire* just four months earlier, Baldwin was able to attract some notice from the nation's attorney general. After an initial breakfast meeting with Kennedy at his home in suburban Virginia, Baldwin helped arrange a secret meeting two weeks later in New York City for Kennedy to meet "Negroes other Negroes [would] listen to."[15]

A motley crew of largely New York–based black artists, actors, some of Baldwin's varied friends and family, and the twenty-five-year-old freedom rider Jerome Smith all met privately with the younger Kennedy. When the meeting began, Kennedy quickly admonished the group for its impatience and for what he saw as black people's distinct lack of gratitude for the administration's multiple efforts for civil rights. As Kennedy scolded the gathering and chided those attracted to the rhetoric of "radical" groups like the Nation of Islam for creating "real trouble" for the administration's efforts with Congress, Smith disrupted the meeting and cut Kennedy off in midsentence. "You don't have no idea what trouble is," Smith snapped, "because I'm close to the moment where I'm ready to take up a gun." The young Smith had been on the first Freedom Ride into Mississippi and the recipient of multiple beatings in attempts to integrate bus facilities there and could no longer abide Kennedy's patronizing attitude. Seeing the tension rise in the room, Baldwin egged on the young Freedom Rider. When Baldwin asked whether the young Jerome Smith would ever fight as a soldier overseas for a country that denied him full citizenship, Smith answered sharply: "Never! Never!" Stunned by his apparent lack of patriotism, Kennedy lectured the group about the suffering of Irish immigrants and pointed to his own family's success and assured them that a black man could be president in forty years or so. Baldwin responded that while a Kennedy could already be president, the "black man" who had been here long before the most recent migration of the Irish to the United States was still "required to supplicate and beg you for justice." The meeting quickly degenerated from there.[16]

In his later television interview with Clark, Baldwin, still apparently angry with Kennedy, mentioned the attorney general on the air and questioned whether the administration had any real moral commitment to the then-current black freedom movement. As Baldwin told Clark: "One has got to force, somehow, from Washington, a moral commitment, not to Negro people, but to the life of this country." During the course of the interview, Baldwin framed the "Negro question" as a problem of white identity and pathology rather than around by-now pedestrian notions of black pathology. "The problem now," Baldwin told his predominantly white television audience, "is how are you going to save yourselves?" When the interview concluded, Baldwin made sure his audience knew the depth of white pathology:

> What white people have to do is try to find out in their own hearts why it was necessary to have a nigger in the first place. Because I'm not a nigger, I am a man, but if you think I'm a nigger, it means you need it. . . . If I'm not the nigger here and if you invented him—you, the white people, invented him, then you've got to find out why. And the future of the country depends on that.[17]

In reframing America's long-standing "race" problem into a question of white identity, Baldwin's political and moral rhetoric, always infused with a sense of the apocalypse, now found its central emphasis. Baldwin saw the United States and the West teetering on the edge of ruin because of white people's willful ignorance. Just several months after the publication of *Fire*, Baldwin's judgment rhetoric lost its impersonal quality and became more specific. The probable cause of the coming catastrophe was now clear. White pathology would usher in sure destruction. By the 1970s and 1980s, disillusioned by King's murder and the urban upheavals that followed, Baldwin's language only became more and more stark in his denunciations of whiteness and white privilege. As Baldwin said to *Essence* magazine in 1984, just a few years before his death: "they debased and defamed themselves and have brought humanity to the edge of oblivion: because they think they are white."[18]

This more personal analysis of white pathology that began shortly after the publication of *Fire*, as demonstrated so clearly in Clark's interview, continued in the large public lectures Baldwin gave throughout the sixties that made up a part of his celebrity involvement in the civil rights movement. In his lectures, Baldwin presented whiteness not as a meaningful racial category but as a bad moral choice. After an impassioned lecture at Kalamazoo College during the mid-1960s, a white teacher in the crowd asked Baldwin about what the role of the white liberal should be in the broader movement for human rights. After calling white liberals "one of our afflictions," Baldwin continued:

> The role of the white liberal in my fight is the role of missionaries, of "I'm trying to help you, you poor black thing you." The thing is — *we're* not in trouble. *You* are. I'd like to suggest that white people turn this around and ask what *white* people can do to help *themselves*. No white liberal knows what Ray Charles is singing about. So how can you help *me*? Work with yourself.[19]

This confrontational stance toward the white world was not reserved only for television interviews and public speeches. Like the angel of death who confronts every individual with the threat of damnation at the end of life, Baldwin challenged his white liberal companions with a fervor barely contained within his slight black body. "I toted *your* barge, baby, I picked *your* cotton," Baldwin often raged in small dinner parties hosted by white friends and associates. "I nursed *your* babies [and] *you* killed my children," he would roar, indicting his bohemian companions who were already bedeviled with white guilt.[20] Often, the sometimes inebriated Baldwin would turn suddenly at the self-important remark so prevalent at these types of gatherings and change from a fun-loving, hard-drinking partygoer to the Jeremiah of old and snap accusingly at a white companion, "[W]here were you the day Martin [King] was shot?" His sharply confrontational questions stunned his white hosts and occasionally precipitated emotional and tearful breakdowns. Baldwin often left his white companions emotionally undone and quivering before his fury, as he demanded that they confront their personal complicity in white supremacy and their investment in a white identity that fostered a destructive lack of self-awareness and false innocence.[21]

"His white acquaintances, in particular," as David Leeming, one Baldwin biographer describes, "were his congregation — listening to his preaching, serving as his witnesses, and directly suffering his anger." He handed out numerous "assignments" to his "disciples," once telling them to rewrite the Gettysburg Address to reflect the contemporary situation. And this "white congregation," both in the dinner parties and on the world stage, was just like his first captive audiences in Harlem storefront churches.[22] Baldwin challenged, confronted, and ushered members of both sets of "congregations" — black first and then white—toward the emotional release typically promised by the salvation offered in evangelical churches.

For Baldwin, the patronizing attitude of the attorney general demonstrated the smug arrogance of white liberals and hinted at the deep reluctance many would feel in facing and confronting white privilege. At the core of this reluctance was an attitude that many whites exhibited that they, as Baldwin writes in *Fire*, had "some intrinsic value" beyond power and resources "that black people need, or want." This attitude, Baldwin believes, is demonstrated in how many of these critics seem to hinge all solutions to racial strife on how fast black people "accept and adopt white standards." Baldwin takes Kennedy's "assurance that a Negro can become President in forty years" as a perfect demonstration of this attitude. In short, Baldwin asserts: "The only thing white people have that black people need, or should want, is power."[23]

Of course, power and privilege are not easily given up. And Baldwin dramatizes this difficulty in his play *Blues for Mister Charlie*, produced in the period right after the publication of *Fire*, when the nature of white pathology was central in Baldwin's thinking and artistic endeavors. Midway through the play, Parnell, a white liberal reporter, pleads patience from a black preacher who is the father of a son brutally murdered by a white shopkeeper. He attempts to explain why he will not confront the murderer: "Meridian—when I asked for mercy a moment ago—I meant—please—please try to understand that it is not so easy to leap over fences, to give things up—all right, to surrender privilege! But if you were among the privileged you would know what I mean. It's not a matter of trying to hold *on;* the things, the privilege—are part of you, are *who* you are. It's in the *gut.*"[24] This passage demonstrates that even before his profound disillusionment after King's assassination, Baldwin held a deep distrust in white people's ability to confront their own culpability in white supremacy and black disfigurement. From early on, Baldwin demanded that white people reject the moral choice of whiteness and become black—prefiguring the exhortations of James Cone and the black theology movement of the late 1960s and early 1970s that shook the theological academy. In order to be "released" from the moral claim black people have, Baldwin councils white people "to become black" and to "become a part of that suffering" they now watch.[25] This language mirrors that of Cone, the most influential voice of the black theological movement who also urged whites to become black. As Cone writes: "Reconciliation to God means that white people are prepared to deny themselves (whiteness), take up the cross (blackness) and follow Christ (black ghetto)." For Cone blackness is not simply a racial category but an expression of moral commitment. "To be black," Cone writes, "means that your heart, your soul, your mind, and your body are where the dispossessed are."[26]

Even with this focus on black suffering, Baldwin acknowledges in one of his writings the suffering of immigrant groups and the arguments Kennedy made at their meeting together. "The Irish middle passage," Baldwin writes, "was as foul as my own, and as dishonorable on the part of those responsible for it." But in this writing he also describes the treacherous moral choices many Irish Americans and other white ethnics made when they arrived on American shores. As Baldwin writes,

> But the Irish became white when they got here and began rising in the world, whereas I became black and began sinking. The Irish . . . had absolutely no choice but to make certain that I could not menace their safety or status or identity: and, if I came too close, they could, with the consent of the governed, kill me. Which means that we can be friendly with each other anywhere in the world, except Boston.[27]

Considering the violence that occurred in Boston over busing in the struggle to integrate public schools during the 1970s, Baldwin's comments have a certain resonance.

In other essays written during the same period, Baldwin explores how the Irish, along with German, Italian, Polish and Jewish immigrants, all became white over time. "No one was white before he/she came to America," Baldwin explains. "It took generations, and a vast amount of coercion, before his became a white country." Whiteness then depended on a certain degree of coercion and exploitation of black people. In Baldwin's words, "America became white" because people need to find ways of "justifying Black subjugation." For Baldwin, whiteness was a socially constructed identity that represented "moral choice" because in fact "there are no white people." It is a choice most non-blacks have had that entraps those who choose it even as it grants a certain degree of privilege. "By deciding that they were white," white people forced themselves into what Baldwin calls a "terrible paradox" where "those who believed that they could control and define Black people divested themselves of the power to control and define themselves."[28]

When Baldwin describes the nature and history of white social identity, he anticipates contemporary scholarship on whiteness that currently wrestles with how white privilege as a legacy of slavery has disrupted the building of political coalitions between the white working class and black people since the Civil War.[29] Baldwin in fact echoes and personalizes the work of Du Bois, who initiated this work over a century ago with his revolutionary *Black Reconstruction*, which transformed the scholarly study of the American Reconstruction period and prefigured the plethora of recent studies on white identity. In the words of one literary critic, Baldwin "revises" Du Bois, who famously stressed "the problem of the color-line" as it relates to blackness and color and defines the contemporary period. As Marlon Ross writes:

> For Baldwin, it is not "the strange meaning of being black" that is the "problem of the Twentieth Century," nor even "the problem of the color-line." Baldwin makes the central problem of the twentieth century the strange meaning of being white, as a structure of feeling within the self and within history—a structure of experience that motivates and is motivated by other denials.[30]

While Ross may be correct, I would argue that Baldwin in fact extends rather than revises Du Bois's reputed focus on blackness. Both Baldwin and Du Bois invoke judgment rhetoric when confronted with white pathology. With his famous "A Litany of Atlanta," published shortly after the race riots in Georgia, where white mobs killed scores of blacks based on rumors of black sexual predators, Du Bois demands that God judge harshly the white perpetrators of injustice. "How long shall the mounting flood of innocent blood roar in Thine ears and pound in our hearts for vengeance?" Du Bois demands of God, "[Instead], pile the pale frenzy of blood-crazed brutes, who do such deeds, high on Thine Altar, Jehovah Jireh, and burn it in hell forever and forever!"[31] The rhetoric Du Bois uses here clearly echoes the judgment rhetoric of enslaved Africans. Here, Du Bois's speech, like Baldwin's, actually makes slaves' implicit calls for retribution against white exploiters more explicit. In addition, the language Du Bois and Baldwin employ grapples more openly with how recent the invention of whiteness truly is. It is a social identity created less than four centuries ago and tied to one of the greatest transfers of wealth in human history: the unpaid, stolen labor of millions of enslaved Africans into the coffers of a small Western elite that still manages largely to dominate the globe.

Baldwin's signal contribution is not the revision of Du Bois's insights but a translation of his ideas about the nature of white social identity into a familial framework that acknowledges the blood relationship between whites and blacks where colonial masters live side by side with those they exploit. Baldwin recognizes that the closeness of these two groups suggests a near-biological connection that is then actualized in the sexual predatory instincts of white planters who in the end produce progeny of mixed heritage. Baldwin then seeks not only to acknowledge these familial connections but also to embrace them as he explores the psychological underpinnings of white attempts, clothed in a false innocence, to deny the reality of their often-biological kinship with the black population of the United States. In one of his last essays before his death, Baldwin states this truth as a simple statement of fact: "We are all androgynous

. . . male in female, female in male, white in black and black in white. We are part of each other. Many countrymen appear to find this fact exceedingly inconvenient and even unfair, and so, very often do I. But none of us can do anything about it."[32]

Ultimately, Baldwin apprehends this complex mesh of blood and denial that makes up whiteness almost totally through the lenses of the familial and the personal. In his conversations with the white elite at the houses of government, the universities, and swank dinner parties, Baldwin renders white social identity in starkly personal and psychological terms. Within these conversations with power, Baldwin describes the false and willful innocence that characterizes whiteness with its adult pretensions to a childlike purity. In making a show of innocence, those who cling to this white social identity fail to communicate true purity; they manage only to verify their guilt and reveal the stench at the center of white identity. In *Fire*, Baldwin condemns "well-meaning people" who proclaim their innocence even as they create conditions for black youth "not very far removed from those described for us by Charles Dickens." Baldwin tells us that it is simply "not permissible" for these "authors of devastation" to be innocent. Indeed, Baldwin bemoans, "It is the innocence which constitutes the crime."[33]

Despite his general suspicion of psychotherapy, Baldwin's analysis of whiteness cuts with a psychological edge.[34] Baldwin combines this with his tendency for apocalyptic language of the preacher determined to save as many souls as possible to paint a psychological portrait of who would become white Americans. From his perspective whiteness represents a kind of narcissism — a false innocence built on selfishness — that inexorably leads to self-destruction and widespread mayhem for a world where we are all "part of each other."[35] Baldwin takes the measure of the scope and destructiveness of whiteness and sees the beginnings of this mass narcissism from within the private psyches of European settlers terrified of "their private selves" who then act "to safeguard their purity."[36] Baldwin's emphasis on purity certainly resonates with the history of racial formation in the United States, where, over time, the "one drop rule" — that is, any discernable amount of African ancestry — determined whether persons were categorized as black.[37] In *Tell Me How Long*, Baldwin refers quite explicitly to the inane one-drop rule through the voice of Leo's brother when Caleb says, "Our mama is *almost* white . . . but that don't make her white. You got to be *all* white to be white."[38] But as always, Baldwin presents this purity that parades as innocence with a personal force within a familial context that combines the moral, the apocalyptic, and the psychological.

This curious combination is what marks Baldwin's early work where he serves as an interpreter of the black experience to a white liberal literary elite in New York during the late 1940s. Baldwin consistently wed the black holiness culture that was his heritage with the psychological sophistication needed for the bohemian elite he often wrote for. This energy would later allow Baldwin to reach a broad audience of concerned whites challenged by the increasing fervor of the civil rights movement, even as he prodded guilt-ridden liberals with his apocalyptic moral language for more action. As Baldwin writes in his introductory notes for *Blues for Mister Charlie:*

> What is ghastly and really almost hopeless in our racial situation now is that the crimes we have committed are so great and so unspeakable that the acceptance of this knowledge would lead, literally, to madness. The human being, then, in order to protect himself, closes his eyes, compulsively repeats his crimes, and enters a spiritual darkness which no one can describe.[39]

Here Baldwin uses a technique that he used extensively in *Notes of a Native Son* more than a decade before. He obscures his own position in America's racial hierarchy as a black man and adopts a literary perspective that assumes the position of the white majority.[40] From this vantage point Baldwin proceeds from within a white identity to dismantle the psychological underpinnings of white supremacy. He first acknowledges the ignorance of the benefactors of white supremacy even as he simultaneously suggests that this ignorance is self-imposed in an insidious effort to avoid any real sense of culpability. But even as this self-imposed ignorance springs from an understandable instinct for self-preservation, this same instinct that so defines the psychological architecture of white supremacy can only bring more disfigurement for black victims and the eventual destruction of the very soul and humanity of many white people who currently benefit from the status quo.

The self-protective act that seeks to avoid any culpability only promotes further actions that will call for yet more culpability. Such an analysis of the addictive, self-destructive qualities that reside in white privilege can only come from a long-standing, intimate conversation with power and intimate knowledge of what Baldwin once called the "weight" of white people on the world — that is, both on individuals and on the broader social and economic reality. As Baldwin diagnoses the sickness of white privilege he suggests how little hope there truly is for those who suffer from this addiction to power. It becomes clear as he becomes more and more disillusioned that Baldwin increasingly sees white people and the America they dominate as doomed. As he asks God through the voice of a grieving minister in *Blues:* "What hope is there for a people who deny their deeds and disown their kinsmen and who do so in the name of purity and love, in the name of Jesus Christ?"[41]

"The Weight of White People in the World"

In one of Baldwin's most famous early essays, "Notes of a Native Son," he discusses his own intimate relationship with the social phenomenon of whiteness. With his father's untimely death, Baldwin could see the impact of white supremacy in the wreckage of his father's life. As Baldwin writes, "When he died I had been away from home for a little over a year. In that year I had had time to become aware of the meaning of all my father's bitter warnings, had discovered the secret of his proudly pursed lips and rigid carriage: I had discovered the weight of white people in the world."[42] This passionate concern for the "weight of white people" and his exploration of white identity and pathology in America began in fact well before his noted confrontation with Robert Kennedy that made the front pages of the *New York Times*. Baldwin's early reflections began in the wake of his father's "bitter warnings" about and deep distrust for white people who always seemed to be "welfare workers" or "bill collectors." When these white persons arrived at the Baldwin household, David Baldwin's temper would boil while his "stiff" posture and "harsh" politeness conveyed "that he felt their very presence in his home to be a violation."[43]

Even as David Baldwin despised white people, he also gave them great deference and in this deference he gave his young son Jimmy early cause to despise his father. When his teacher Orilla Miller offered to take the young Jimmy to the theater, not knowing that the theater, like other worldly activities, was forbidden for the Baldwin children, she had a meeting with David Baldwin in an effort to convince him of its educational value. Even though the young Jimmy wanted to go, his father's obeisance to a white woman he had scorned just moments before her arrival made Jimmy deeply ashamed of his father and his sudden bout of humiliating cowardice. "It was clear . . . that my father was agreeing very much against his will and that he would have refused permission if he had dared," Baldwin writes. "The fact that he did not dare," Baldwin continues, "caused me to despise him."[44] This early discovery of his father's impotence before white status illustrates how Baldwin from the beginning of his writing career always seemed to recognize how whiteness and white privilege hold a fearful attraction to both blacks and whites in America. In the person of his father, Baldwin experienced firsthand, in flesh and blood, how the "weight" and presence of whiteness distorted blacks' sense of themselves and their own beauty. David Baldwin had the regal bearing of an "African tribal chieftain." In his son's words: "he was black," but he "did not know that he was beautiful."[45]

Hints of Baldwin's future analysis of whiteness as the self-deluded desire and attempt for what is a false innocence are present in his earliest nonfiction writings. In one essay, Baldwin quite clearly claims that the "dehumanization of the Negro" was indivisible from the "dehumanization" and the "loss" in "identity" of the white majority.[46] But, remarkably, the first literary portrayal of the dangers of self-delusion and false innocence that Baldwin would later identify with "whiteness" is in his depiction of the black father and minister Gabriel in *Go Tell It*. Gabriel's story demonstrates not only the shaky ethical foundation conversion-based religion often rests upon (as discussed in chapter 2), but it also shows how destructive a false sense of innocence can be. Gabriel, convinced of his own righteousness, impregnates his mistress and leaves her to cope with her pregnancy alone. Even after she dies, Gabriel refuses to see his own culpability.

Baldwin's depiction of the dangers of self-delusion continued in his next novel, *Giovanni's Room*. Gabriel's spiritual heir on the path to self-destruction is most assuredly David, who, in a novel where all the major characters are white, becomes the early template for Baldwin's description of the white identity as essentially built on a destructive self-delusion clothed in innocence. David, a white American expatriate in Paris who is already "engaged" to a fellow American traveling through Spain without him, becomes sexually involved with an Italian man, Giovanni. Because he refuses to love fully his new companion despite his keen desire to, he rejects Giovanni and indirectly causes, or so David believes, Giovanni's death. This death overshadows David and frames the novel, punctuating its beginning and end. David's notion of masculinity imprisons him and limits his ability to see love where he does not expect to. As he tells Giovanni during their breakup at the climax of the novel: "But I'm a man . . . a man! What do you think can *happen* between us?"[47]

Because of homophobia, particularly that engendered by the various black cultural nationalists who shaped early black literary theory in the 1970s, Baldwin's work in *Giovanni's Room* has been overlooked. Often critics enamored with his engagement of race have generally seen Baldwin's second novel, in which every major character is white, as his "gay" book and as an unfortunate "detour" from his concerns with racial identity.[48] Since the characters are white, Baldwin's second effort is assumed to have little to say about race. And many believe that to be white in the United States is to be without race. But, in fact, throughout his "white" and "gay" novel supposedly empty of racial concerns, Baldwin, in the words of one critic, "refers to color and racial characteristics constantly as a way of locating the cultural situation of the characters."[49] Baldwin does in fact introduce David on the very first page with a reference to his whiteness and to his ancestral connections as a white American with the first European immigrants who brutally conquered the New World. Speaking in David's voice, Baldwin writes, "My ancestors conquered a continent, pushing across death-laden plains, until they came to an ocean which faced away from Europe into a darker past."[50] This focus on David in Baldwin's second novel can be seen, as some have suggested, as the flip slide of his exploration in *Go Tell It*. An early critic and biographer asserts that Baldwin's first book tells of "the black condition," while the second explains "how this [condition] had come about by the self-deception of the privileged."[51]

Baldwin's portrayal of David, in fact, prefigures his later explorations into white identity in his nonfiction essays. It models the very essence of how whiteness as a social identity is built on self-deception where public protests of innocence allow people to evade the truth of their own destructiveness. Baldwin defines David early in the novel through his reluctance to examine and know himself. Before David confesses this lack of self-awareness, he describes in general terms what shapes a life of privilege and how the presumptions of the "self-made" person mark his own life and demonstrate his firm connections to status and power. "For I am—or I was—one of those people who pride themselves on their willpower," David tells us. "[But] people who believe that they are strong-willed and the masters of their destiny can only continue to believe this by becoming specialists in self-deception."[52] Privilege, Baldwin believes, only continues where it is unacknowledged; the willful innocence that characterizes privilege can only be sustained where there is a lack of self-examination.

David's story surely illustrates how this lack of self-awareness shapes and reinforces privilege. David confesses early in the novel that he had "decided to allow no room in the universe for something which shamed and frightened me." And he succeeded in this endeavor, in his words, "by not looking at the universe, by not looking at myself, by remaining, in effect, in constant motion."[53] Because his father is willing to support him as he travels through Europe, David is free to engage in this frenetic activity that obscures his self-loathing and his lack of purpose. In short, privilege finances his slow self-immolation and fosters the exact opposite of the self-awareness his father assumes he will achieve on his trip to Europe. Early on, David demonstrates how self-deception and self-loathing shape all of his intimate encounters. When he first meets a potential lover in Paris, David turns away and admits that "the contempt" he feels for the man actually "involved" a measure of his own "self-contempt."[54]

As David becomes involved with Giovanni, he does not have the courage to love fully and gain the self-awareness he needs to escape his self-contempt. As his relationship with Giovanni grows, David cannot bear the vulnerability that love demands. When David talks with a shared friend, Jacques, who challenges David not to be "safe" and to have the courage to both give and receive love, David recoils in shame at the prospect of his potential love of Giovanni. Jacques accuses David with a Baldwin-like passion of rejecting love because David sees his love for Giovanni as dirty. Jacques assures him, "[Y]ou can make your time together anything but dirty; you can give each other something which will make both of you better—forever—if you will *not* be ashamed, if you will only *not* play it safe." But there are consequences to playing it safe. Indeed, love from Baldwin's perspective subverts ugliness, dirtiness, and shame, but David in his refusal to risk and step out of his privileged innocence will, as Jacques tells him, "end up trapped" in his "own dirty body, forever."[55]

In rejecting Giovanni, David rejects his own body and self he so despises. And when David's fiancée leaves him after discovering him in a gay bar, he is forced to face all alone the reality of Giovanni's death. It is then that David realizes the truth of Jacques's prophecy. He loses his innocence in a flash, but, of course, now it is too late for Giovanni and for him. David's recognition of this loss of innocence comes like nearly all revelations do for Baldwin's characters: with an anguish that is akin to what a young Jimmy experienced on the floor of Mother Horn's church. As *Giovanni's Room* closes, David looks in the mirror and does not like what he sees:

> The body in the mirror forces me to turn and face it. And I look at my body, which is under sentence of death. It is lean, hard, and cold, the incarnation of mystery. And I do not know what moves in this body, what this body is searching. It is trapped in my mirror as it is trapped in time and it hurries toward revelation.
>
> *When I was a child, I spake as a child, I understood as a child, I thought as a child: but when I became a man, I put away childish things.*[56]

Like John in *Go Tell It*, the revelation that comes destroys innocence and ushers those burdened with awful knowledge into adulthood. In its terrible wake this revelation makes David's own body a stranger to him in ways that echo how John's body was caught on the threshing floor before the invading presence of God. And even as Baldwin ends with a portion from a famous biblical passage that celebrates the nature of love even as it marks the end of childhood, readers realize that David's keen determination to retain his sense of innocence will leave him an empty man.

What we find in Baldwin's two essays in *Fire* is an extension of the themes of shame and self-delusion that animate *Giovanni's Room* away from simply a psychological terrain confined to the self to broader political analysis that encompasses the larger culture and society; it makes the transition from interior, even spiritual language to a bracingly outward political rhetoric. These themes are now explored on a canvas that is at once more directly personal and much larger in scope and ambition. Baldwin had examined in his essays before *Fire* the ways in which anxiety and self-loathing have animated sexual expression in the West, especially in the context of disfigured and abused black bodies. With these essays in *Fire,* Baldwin brings a personal edge and new life to this same concern as he explicitly writes of how his own sexual anxiety helped lead him to the point where he was overcome in the presence of a white god. In a similar manner, Baldwin frames his prophetic appeal to white liberals through a consideration of how a self-deluded innocence can only bring destruction and grief. Baldwin in this instance reprises an old theme from his fiction and translates his interest from Giovanni's small room in France to the much larger canvas of race in America. In an essay about Norman Mailer written a year before *Fire,* Baldwin had already pushed the analysis implicit in *Giovanni's Room* toward a broader conversation about race, self-delusion, and power. But as the 1960s only became more tumultuous, Baldwin saw that clinging to white identity was a simple denial of historical consciousness that could only bring the very end of history.

American Innocence, White Privilege, and the End of History

Many scholars have focused on Baldwin's reflections on exile and how this shaped an American innocence that drew on his appropriation of the language and themes of Henry James. But perhaps what James most offered Baldwin was a language with which to talk about what he felt were the two dominant markers for the (white) American personality: freedom and innocence. In an interview with his one-time secretary and future biographer, David Leeming, Baldwin describes James as "the only American writer" who had some sense of what Baldwin termed "the American Dilemma." For Baldwin this dilemma was illustrated in James's greatest novels, which focus on a "certain inability to perceive the reality of others." Baldwin adapts this notion to white Americans' inability to see their black blood relations. As Baldwin tells Leeming: "It's a failure to see, failure to live, a failure to be. Americans do not see me when they look at me, their kinsman—literally blood of their blood, created by them. The price they pay for living is to pretend I'm not here." This failure to see is linked most profoundly perhaps with a supposed innocence that in Baldwin's terms is "the failure to touch, to see." It is this supposed innocence—this self-delusion—that traps the David of *Giovanni's Room.* He is trapped as Baldwin tells Leeming "because he lied to himself about something sacred—because he wanted to remain innocent."[57]

Baldwin presses for nothing less than innocence's end because it is the only way for Americans to have what they often celebrate with empty pious phrases: that is real freedom—freedom that accepts responsibility. "The end of innocence," he says, "means you've finally entered the picture. And it means that you'll accept consequences too."[58] And central to this acceptance in Baldwin's view is the embrace of a historical consciousness that black people have already been forced to embrace. To be a "custodian of an inheritance" is to accept a freedom, which recognizes that true human connection goes beyond property and wealth and fully engages the horrors of the past. A lack of historical consciousness is what marks white pathology. As one critic writes, "Baldwin speaks of white guilt as a 'personal incoherence' and suggests that history is the site of white Americans' psychic entrapment."[59] What makes history such a compelling factor, Baldwin writes in an essay written in 1965, is that "we carry it within us, are unconsciously controlled by it in many ways." In short: "history is literally *present* in all that we do."[60] Baldwin demands that those seduced by the dream of whiteness see that their supposed innocence is in fact a denial of a history marked by inequality and trouble. But Baldwin understands that those with power usually evade any sense of history that may demonstrate how they have unfairly come to achieve the privilege they now hold. In their evasion they write their own false history. As Baldwin writes in his last novel: "written history is, and must be, merely the vocabulary of power, and power is history's most seductively attired false witness."[61]

In addition to this lack of historical consciousness, Baldwin believes that many white elites, no matter how good their intentions, have a naive understanding of power and alienation. Many black people, on the other hand, have an understanding of alienation in their flesh and bodies in ways adherents to existentialism, Freudian psychology, and Marxism could only theorize about. Baldwin in an *Esquire* portrait of Norman Mailer's peacock behavior recounts an exchange between the two on the nature of power. When Mailer says in passing, "I want to know how power works," Baldwin snaps in reply: "Well, I know how power works, it has worked on me, and if I didn't know how power worked, I would be dead."[62] In addition, Baldwin believes that black people have been forced to grapple with cosmic indifference in ways whites have not. That there are those of European descent who refuse to grapple with this indifference only reveals the breathtaking extent of white arrogance and denial. As Baldwin writes,

> The world had prepared no place for you, and if the world had its way, no place would ever exist. Now, this is true for everyone, but in the case of a Negro, this truth is absolutely naked: if he deludes himself about it, he will die. This is not the way this truth presents itself to white men, who believe the world is theirs and who, albeit unconsciously, expect the world to help them in the achievement of their identity. But the world does not do this—for anyone; the world is not interested in anyone's identity.[63]

Baldwin suggests that if black people "delude" into thinking that the world owes them something—that is, act white—they will self-destruct and meet the same fate as Baldwin's father did; like David Baldwin, they will become steadily more and more detached from reality and lose their sanity before a white god who has refused in the end to return their love. Baldwin understands that black people can become pale reflections of their white counterparts whose supposed innocence transforms them into frightful creatures trapped in a self-imposed prison of purity where their inner deadness inflects damage on everyone else. As Baldwin warns quite starkly in one early essay: anybody who "insists on remaining in a state of innocence long after innocence is dead" will turn into "a monster" that invites its own destruction.[64]

But despite this demand to see the world as it is without God, Baldwin himself holds to a posture deeply informed by the religious tradition he seemed at first to reject. Even with his continued intimations that a frightful end was surely coming for a society addicted to whiteness, violence, and domination, Baldwin still believed in a New Jerusalem. Perhaps this new city would be made with human hands and not supernatural ones, but Baldwin, despite his own calls for a secular judgment, believed in the possibility of a new sacred reality. Toward the end of his life in one of his last interviews, Baldwin confessed to Richard Goldstein: "I am working toward the New Jerusalem. That's true, I'm not joking. I won't live to see it but I do believe in it. I think we're going to be better than we are."[65]

Epilogue

"A Bastard People"

blackness, exile, and the
possibilities of redemption

Behind them was the darkness, nothing but the darkness, and all around them destruction, and before them nothing but the fire — a bastard people, far from God, singing and crying in the wilderness.

<small>GO TELL IT ON THE MOUNTAIN, *1953*</small>

B aldwin's "habit," in the words of his first serious biographer, "of referring to himself as though he were the personification of his race" sometimes edged from the provocative into the absurd.[1] Despite his distrust and unease with city life and his later residence in southern France far outside the Parisian metropolis, Baldwin was the quintessential urban denizen (especially in those early years spent primarily in New York and Paris). And, it is quite shocking that this city boy would transform himself before predominantly white audiences at dinner parties and various universities into the role of the archetypal black man among the rural folk who toiled away in the service of white southern planters. Even though Baldwin, of course, had not set foot in the cotton fields of the southern countryside until his thirties, it did not prevent him at Cambridge University from raging before more than a thousand students: "I picked the cotton . . . [and] I carried it to market. I built the railways under someone else's whip—for nothing, for nothing! The Southern oligarchy was created by *my* labour, *my* sweat, the violation of *my* children—all this in the land of the free and the home of the brave."[2]

Fortunately, Baldwin consistently used facets of his life in more illuminating ways to highlight aspects of the black experience in the United States. Baldwin, for example, often used his status as a "bastard" to describe the marginal position of black people relative to mainstream Western culture. Baldwin throughout his career married the celebratory impulses of a liberalism animated by notions of American exceptionalism with the deep suspicions that characterized a black nationalism, which saw the continued subjugation of black people as intrinsic to any notion of an American identity. "The whole American reality," Baldwin tells Quincy Troupe in one of his last recorded interviews, "is based on the necessity of keeping Black people out of it."[3] At the same time, since his earliest essays, Baldwin has described black people in the United States as quintessentially American. In "Many Thousands Gone," he writes, "Negroes are Americans and their destiny is the country's destiny."[4] Given these two realities, Willie Walker is quite convincing when he argues in his recent dissertation that Baldwin "was both black cultural nationalist and American exceptionalist, both a rejectionist of American founding ideals, and a proponent of the idea that African Americans were thoroughly American peoples."[5] In this, Walker unravels what Baldwin means (or comes to mean) when he writes, "He [the black person] is not a visitor to the West, but a citizen there, and American; as American as the Americans who despise him."[6]

By using his own marginal status as a bastard, Baldwin works within the tension between tepid liberalism and a rigid black nationalism that animates some of his best work, to embrace the familial pain at the heart of the relationship of blacks and whites in America. Bastard as a metaphor points quite naturally toward the black self-hatred that Baldwin understood as intrinsic to a black people's appropriation of a far distant white god. Gabriel in *Go Tell It* disdainfully describes black people as a bastard people who press toward a god who does not answer. They press, it seems, simply because they have no alternative. There is nowhere else for this displaced people to go and no one else to rely upon in the silence of night as their ancient gods are eclipsed in the rigors of the Middle Passage and a brutal enslavement. As Baldwin writes in Gabriel's voice, "Behind them was the darkness, nothing but the darkness, and all around them destruction, and before them nothing but the fire." These people, Gabriel says, are "a bastard people, far from God, singing and crying in the wilderness!"[7] Whether or not Gabriel is right that they were far from the Christian god is unclear, but they were, in fact, far from a home where their ancestral gods had been and now they had only their songs and their transported rhythms to keep them company.

For Baldwin, to be "a bastard people" is to be an exilic people who sing and cry in the wilderness. The famous question of the 137th Psalm is the favorite biblical text of Baldwin's preaching father and embodies this sense of exile: "How can I sing the Lord's song in a strange land?"[8] In *Blues for Mister Charlie*, Baldwin takes this biblical fragment of youthful memory and uses it to define black people's harried existence in the "New World." In the second act, Meridian, the preacher whose son is brutally murdered at the beginning of the play, begins his prayer before his congregation with a confession: "My heart is heavier than it has ever been before." And then he cries aloud to God:

Everyone under the sound of my voice and many more souls than that, feel as I feel, and tremble as I tremble, and bleed as I bleed. It is not that the days are dark—we have known dark days. It is not only that the blood runs down and no man helps us; it is not only that our children are destroyed before our eyes. It is not only that our lives, from day to day and every hour of each day, are menaced by the people among whom you have set us down. We have borne all these things, my Lord, and we have done what the prophets of old could not do, we have sung the Lord's song in a strange land. In a strange land! What was the sin committed by our forefathers in the time that has vanished on the other side of the flood, which has had to be expiated by chains, by the lash, by hunger and thirst, by slaughter, by fire, by the rope, by the knife, and for so many generations, on these wild shores, in this strange land? Our offense must have been mighty, our crime immeasurable. But it is not the past which makes our hearts so heavy. It is the present. Lord, where is our hope?[9]

Meridian's deep questioning about where hope could possibly exist is all the more poignant in view of the vast litany of sufferings he has just recounted for God's attention. But what catches him short later in his prayer is not simply the suggestion that black people's sinfulness caused these troubles, but rather the earnest questions of the young who ask which way to turn. Before their questions, Meridian does not have any answers. As Meridian prays: "Now, when the children come, my Lord, and ask which road to follow, my tongue stammers and my heart fails." But in the end, although he continues to grapple with what to tell the younger generation and his prayers appear to go unanswered, Meridian affirms to his god his place in the United States: "I will not abandon the land—this strange land, which is my home."[10] In this complicated strangeness and alienation that a silent white god imposes on black worshipers, where black separatism and the return to Africa are not seen as viable options, Baldwin's use of bastard as a metaphor suggests the pain, alienation, inner exile that come with a loss of identity. And this loss, of course, is one that can never be fully rectified. In one essay written a few years before his death, Baldwin describes how bereft black Americans feel "in the midnight hour" while their "missing identity aches." The drift brought with the trauma of the Middle Passage is never overcome. "One is mysteriously shipwrecked forever," Baldwin writes, "in the Great New World."[11] Bastards are always in a state of personal exile; they may never know their true biological fathers and they consequently may never feel accepted.

In effect, Baldwin transposes Ralph Ellison's theme of invisibility as explored in his seminal *The Invisible Man* into the familial relationship of unwed fathers to the children they refuse to recognize as their own. But even as he lauds Ellison's work, Baldwin would criticize his central theme of opacity. Baldwin calls Ellison and his fellow traveler, Albert Murray, "gifted writers" who are "trapped in the same way." As Baldwin tells Quincy Troupe: "*The Invisible Man* is fine as far as it goes until you ask yourself who's invisible to whom? You know, what is this dichotomy supposed to do? Are we invisible before each other? And invisible why, and by what system can one hope to be invisible?"[12] Baldwin answers these questions as he transforms the frustrations of opacity into the ache of unrecognized paternity; the unseen becomes the discarded and the unclaimed.

Familial Space in Black and White

Baldwin's biggest complaint against whites begins not with their "willful innocence" but rather with their absolute refusal to see a biological, flesh-and-blood connection between themselves and black people in the United States. As Baldwin writes, "The [race] problem is rooted in the question of how one treats one's flesh and blood, especially one's children. The blacks are the despised and slaughtered children of the great western house—nameless and unnameable bastards."[13] The notion of willful innocence makes sense only in the context of this basic denial, which is the very center of white pathology. "The great dilemma of being a white American precisely is," Baldwin tells one interviewer, "that they deny their only kinship."[14]

Of course, while Baldwin's translation of societal relationship into the smaller more intense frame of personal and familial relations can be provocative and insightful, it is meager in its political scope. This criticism of Baldwin finds its fullest expression in Cornel West's early work *Prophesy Deliverance!* There, West maps out four traditions within black America, which have developed in opposition to white supremacy, each with a different stance toward the redemptive possibilities of black cultural life. West characterizes Baldwin as an exemplar of what he calls the marginalist response whose "basic concern . . . is to loosen the constraints on individuality in Afro-American life" in a critical stance toward both black culture and the broader American society. As West defines it, the marginalist response grapples with the restrictive aspects of black culture and celebrates an individualism that ultimately cripples any larger coherent political program. Baldwin, like others in this marginalist tradition, is "intuitively close to Afro-American culture and simultaneously on the edge of it." As West writes, "Even Baldwin's more vitriolic writings about social change have a deep moral fiber which speaks to the heart of individuals rather than to a community planning to undertake concerted political action."[15]

Indeed, Baldwin sought in part to demonstrate in *Go Tell It* how the religious and decisions of others can dictate and limit the choice of John, his alter ego in the novel. Even as Baldwin warns in his early work, from *Go Tell It* to *Giovanni's Room* and *Another Country*, of the risks of safe havens and easy choices, he celebrates how the individual has the capacity to break the social control of religion and loveless fears of social convention. "I was not born to be defined by someone else," Baldwin says in one interview, "but by myself, and myself only."[16] But this emphasis on the individual yields a cramped notion of freedom limited to seeking the humane and the tender intimacies of personal relationships instead of radical social change. As Baldwin writes: "People who in some sense know who they are can't change the world always, but they can do something . . . to make a life a little more human. Human in the best sense. Human in terms of joy, freedom which is always private, respect, respect for one another, even such things as manners."[17] It is here as much as anywhere that Baldwin's sentimentalism belies all his protests to the contrary. While it is understandable given Baldwin's close association with Henry James that he often seems to equate freedom with escape from a society of manners, it is still regrettable. It only demonstrates how Baldwin's tendency to focus on the interpersonal realm can overwhelm any larger societal concerns he may have.

So even while Baldwin consistently criticizes liberalism for promising a freedom that is dependent on the subjugation of black people, Baldwin's broader artistic vision also has a truly cramped conception of freedom. The principal domain throughout most of his novels remains the tight and the often-dirty personal and domestic spaces of human life. In Baldwin's most successful novels, *Go Tell It* and *Giovanni's Room*, tight dirty rooms help demonstrate the claustrophobia of religion and self-delusion and become the basic terrain where love and adulthood are explored and achieved with decidedly mixed results. Even Baldwin's most overtly political novel, *Tell Me How Long*, as critic Donald Gibson observes, turns on intimacy of familial and romantic connections and how an actor (or any artist) can mediate "the desire for privacy and the necessity of public involvement."[18] As a celebrity writer Baldwin understood this tension. Harried, Baldwin often felt his fame choked the life out of his work, and he was pushed to more and more isolated patches outside the country in order to write beyond the demands of activism. Leo as Baldwin's fictional counterpart captures this tension when he tells a black revolutionary friend, "The only space which means anything to me is the space between myself and other people."[19] His exile, it seems, helped to shape his interest in privacy, family, and intimacy. Baldwin's explorations of the twin dilemmas of race and love, which haunt the very notion of America, are reduced here to what Gibson calls the "political anatomy of space." And although the bastard metaphor surely captures the psychosexual dimensions of white supremacy, a strong economic critique of American society birthed in a sharply racialized context is largely absent. Surely, bastards and their unwed mothers are starved of real material resources beyond these valid but lesser concerns of psychological attachment.

But what West and others have raised is whether the familial images that so dominate Baldwin's rhetoric are broad enough to sustain his collective, societal imagination and ambitions. When Baldwin recounts a conversation he has with Elijah Muhammad in *Fire*, he demonstrates just how much his deep individualism animates his entire literary and social project. During the course of their conversation, Baldwin told the black religious nationalist that he had "left the church twenty years ago" and that he had not joined any other organization since. When Muhammad asked him how he identified himself now, Baldwin refused "to be stampeded" into saying he was Christian and responded at first with "Nothing." On reflection he answered: "I'm a writer. I like doing things alone."[20] Baldwin refused to be "stampeded" into identifying himself with any religious or group perspective that smacks of the tribalism he had always abhorred. But Baldwin was also not comfortable with the alternative he had chosen. He suspected even then that his individualistic humanism was, in his words, "not enough."[21]

Although many of the black nationalists who have criticized Baldwin have been deeply homophobic, they may have been right to criticize the extent to which Baldwin remained cocooned in the very same tepid liberalism he often disparaged. Many scholars writing from a perspective that grapples fully with gay and lesbian perspectives have leveled similar criticisms. William Cohen, for example, sees Baldwin's *Another Country* as endorsing individual values like love by "insistently traversing the racial and sexual lines that have historically bounded" the project of liberal humanism. In doing so, Baldwin attempts to push its "ideology of salvation and love" toward a "revolutionary conception" that challenges liberal ideology on its own terms. But Cohen wonders about the viability of this attempt that cannot even sustain the representation of a black gay subject—"a person simultaneously gay and black"—in its effort to confront the place of race and sex in American society.[22]

Beyond this, however, Baldwin's very use of the term bastard suggests the extent to which he is obsessed with gaining recognition from whites. This obsession might in the end undermine the basis of black unity and black self-regard that is necessary for the pursuit of black equality in a United States whose very existence, as a nation-state, seems predicated on the subjugation of all things and all people black. As much as Baldwin's analysis helps unmask the self-hate deeply endemic in black life, using the term bastard suggests, in the end his desire for recognition trumps nearly everything else. This sense of unrequited love dominates his work almost as much as his concern that black people love themselves and appreciate their own distinct cultural identity in the United States.

Even without this cloying desire for recognition, the term *bastard* is an unwieldy metaphor for black life in the United States. For Baldwin, his absolute fixation on the missing father breeds a silent and poisonous sexism. His focus on unrequited love begins and ends with male anxiety that renders invisible the lives and passions of mothers, wives, and daughters. Baldwin's preoccupation with black men's loss of male privilege—of manhood—silences the voices of women. Audre Lorde, in a conversation recorded in *Essence* magazine for an issue published in 1984, challenged the exclusion of black women from his analysis of white supremacy. She pushed him to redefine black masculinity and confront black men who continued to brutalize the women closest to them. "[W]hat we do have is a real disagreement about your responsibility not just to me but to my son and to our boys," Lorde told a stunned Baldwin. "Your responsibility to him is to get across to him in a way that I never will be able to . . . [and] tell him I'm not a fit target for his fury." Even while Baldwin pleaded with Lorde to recognize that "a Black man has a prick" and that the society sought to "hack it off," Lorde, while noting the specific challenges of black men in contemporary American society, continued to demand the inclusion of women in Baldwin's moral and political calculus. Lorde understood that even as black men may be America's nightmare, black women had not even achieved this dubious honor in American consciousness. "Even worse than the nightmare is the blank," Lorde informed her fellow writer. "And Black women are the blank." So when Baldwin said with a hint of exasperation, "don't you realize that in this republic the only real crime is to be a Black man," Lorde's response was not a surprise: "No, I don't realize that. I realize the only crime is to be Black . . . and that includes me too."[23]

Prefiguring the Decline of Afro-Protestantism

But beyond these calls for the radical inclusion of women that must be honored, the bastard metaphor only works in so far as we can characterize the relationship between the ancestors of black Americans and the Christianity they adopted as one of betrayal. What Baldwin's work suggests is that the black evangelical consensus, if one could ever really call it that, was an uneasy one. Given its full emergence only toward the very end of the nineteenth century under the threat of racial terror and lynching, Baldwin's deep questioning only four to five decades later is not surprising. For literary critic Sondra O'Neale, Baldwin's work is a sign from within the literary world of Christianity's decline as a force within black culture. As she writes,

> Baldwin should be seen as the last black American writer to exploit as a major theme the black man's relationship with Christianity. Conversely, he may be considered the first black American writer to distance himself from the lone enduring black institution, the black church, not by its notable absence . . . but by his overtly persistent portrayal of its lack of authentic Christian commitment. In this and his subsequent treatment of homosexuality as an acceptable form of human love . . . Baldwin opened the floodgate for contemporary anti-Christian, non-biblically based black American literature.[24]

Indeed, the late black Baptist historian James Washington labeled the contemporary era since the early 1980s as a moment noted for "the increasing decline of the moral influence of African-American Christianity."[25]

Although Baldwin augured this moment where Christianity would be a declining influence on the cultural life of black people in the United States, he still was in large measure a creature of black religion and specifically black evangelicalism. In a real sense, Christianity was Baldwin's adopted father that he sometimes despised but still loved. As he told Jordan Elgrably and George Plimpton in an interview, *"Go Tell It on the Mountain* was about my relationship to my father and to the church, which is the same thing really."[26] Baldwin never embraced a non-Christian reality with the assurance and aplomb that noteworthy black science fiction author Octavia Butler does when she writes: "At the moment there are no true aliens in our lives—no Martians, Tau Cetians to swoop down in advanced spaceships, their attentions firmly fixed on the all-important Us, no gods or devils, no spirits, angels, or gnomes. Some of us know this. Deep within ourselves we know it. We're on our own, the focus of no interest except our consuming interest in ourselves."[27]

With Baldwin we have a different creature all together. We cannot help but remember what black mystic Howard Thurman taught—reprising Augustinian wisdom from his own dark body. As Thurman writes: "I asked myself how I may find a clue to God's purposes in the world? How may I sense Him at work? Already I am aware of Him in the hunger of my heart; this is a crucial clue."[28] God, whatever its substantive, external reality is surely not absent from Baldwin's mental horizon. What is present is hunger for the divine married to a hunger for the right. As late as 1984, Baldwin remembers a meeting he had recently with childhood friends. Now clothed in celebrity and some fortune, Baldwin writes, "They still believed in the Lord, but I had quarreled with Him, and offended Him, and walked out of His house."[29]

One can almost feel the texture of Baldwin's long-strained relationship with holiness culture amid a dialogue between Mother Henry and her grandson, the young Richard, whose murder begins the play *Blues for Mister Charlie*. Their conversation is studded with references that suggest various generational shifts and tensions within the black community. The relationships among Richard, his preacher father, Meridian, and his grandmother, Mother Henry, are emblematic of the then-nascent Black Power generation, the religious leadership that was shaped decisively by the depression and the Second World War, and the adherents of old-time religion born right after slavery. During the course of their conversation, Mother Henry shares with the young, angry Richard what she learned from her enslaved parents, who must have been bedeviled constantly with the threat of family breakup; they never knew when a family member would be sold. Mother Henry's parents learned to fight hard to maintain and nurture family ties while keeping a deep reverence for God. Mother Henry tells her wayward grandson that she was determined to take care of her husband and "raise my children in the fear of God." Richard immediately challenges his grandmother with a short "You know I don't believe in God, Grandmama." And Mother Henry responds, perhaps gingerly, "You don't know what you talking about. Ain't no way possible for you not to believe in God. It ain't up to you." But when Richard continues to press his grandmother with, "who's it up to, then?" Mother Henry answers in a way that must have resonated in the inner landscape of Baldwin's secret self: "It's up to the life in you—the life in you. *That* knows where it comes from, *that* believes in God. You doubt me, you just try holding your breath long enough to die."[30] An insulated religious community did not just externally impose a struggle with God on a helpless Baldwin. The struggle with God did not come just from without; it also came from within. Only Baldwin's death in southern France could end this skirmish that began in the streets of Harlem against the Christian god.

But even as Baldwin fought against what he could not in the end fully control, his dynamic struggle reveals a young evangelical consensus within Afro-Protestantism under great stress. This consensus, forged and solidified just a little over a century ago, threatens to buckle beneath the wash of modernity, the continued strain of gross inequality in American society, and the continued subjugation of all things black materially, socially, and culturally in the United States and throughout the world. In retrospect, looking back over several decades of black Christianity's decline, the civil rights movement now seems to represent the last moment when Afro-Protestantism had a decisive impact on the nature and character of black life in the United States. All that seems to remain is a righteous indignation that continues to call America to account and a frenetic music and liturgical life that continues to demonstrate the extent to which black suffering's cultural products can provoke, excite, be marketed and sold, and sometimes even heal.

But while we must respect Baldwin's wishes that he not be "stampeded" into identifying as a Christian, it is clear that the nature of Baldwin's relationship to the church of his youth was real and continued right up to the grave. Even as his work criticizes church culture, his ebullient use of its idioms, energy, and claims for righteousness undermine his critique of the culture of the holiness church that he found so often stultifying. Perhaps this ambiguity in Baldwin's relationship to the black church and Christianity in general is best captured in a scene at the church altar involving the aunt of the protagonist in *Go Tell It.* Aunt Florence, caught between "a terrible longing to surrender and a desire to call God into account," beats her fists on the altar, raging against God's apparent preference for undeserved others even as she has attempted throughout her life "to walk upright" to no effect. Mistaking her anguish against God's unfairness for earnest repentance, sanctified elders looking on her passionate plea urge her on: "Call on Him, daughter!"[31] The ambiguity of the critical response of *The Amen Corner* discussed in the first chapter of this work demonstrates that the insularity and hypocrisy so evident in Baldwin's portrayal of black holiness church culture is not the final word. Baldwin's display of that culture's vigor and compelling energy and beauty continues to convey a powerful sense of the humanity of persons who show in their fervent worship of a god who appears to hate them, a rich humanity filled to the brim with an awe-inspiring, never-ending creative spirit. Despite Florence's abject disappointment and her bitterness toward God, all that outside observers could see is the fervor with which she pursues God and hungers for the right—transforming, in their eyes, her rebuke of a distant deity into her apparent surrender to the burdensome reality of sacred presence. And so it is with Baldwin and many of us.

Afterword

Stubborn Hopes for a New Jerusalem

I will not abandon the land—this strange land, which is my home.

BLUES FOR MISTER CHARLIE, *1964*

W hen I first decided to pursue a project on James Baldwin's life and work, I was convinced that his relationship to Christianity had not been treated with the degree of complexity and seriousness in the scholarly community that it deserved. Although my mother had some of his books scattered along various bookshelves in my childhood home, I had not really encountered Baldwin for myself until my college years. But when I did finally read his first and most polished novel, *Go Tell It on the Mountain,* I found in its pages the same compelling church culture that I had known as a youth. And even though Baldwin's prose in *Go Tell It* sometimes constrains the rhythms of black expressive language with a restrained style that echoes his literary mentor, Henry James, the fevered life that underlies much of black holiness culture still manages to overflow the boundaries of Baldwin's delicate novel. I found great similarities between the lively church culture depicted in Baldwin's first novel and the black holiness worship I witnessed in my aunt's Pentecostal church in Memphis during the 1970s and 1980s.

What is so striking about the fiction and nonfiction essays that follow *Go Tell It* is how decisive Baldwin's religious heritage is in all of his work from the 1940s until his death in the late 1980s. Even as Baldwin fervently embraces the outside, secular world, forever turning his back on the church culture of his youth, he challenges a nation still captive to white supremacy, with a moral rhetoric percolating with language from black holiness culture. Despite this evidence of a continued connection with his religious heritage, many scholars in the past largely ignored Baldwin's fascinating and complicated relationship with religion and only noted in passing its impact on his work and life. Those few published essays that did discuss the matter at any length tended to explore the connection in a somewhat simplistic fashion. And though the few unpublished dissertations that have been written on the subject generally do treat Baldwin's interest in religion much more fully than these few scattered essays, they still do not give a complete and rounded portrait of his engagement with Christianity. They largely fail to render Baldwin's ambiguous posture toward black holiness culture and tend not to treat his ultimate rejection of the Christian god seriously enough.

Despite this relative neglect, the impact of Baldwin's religious heritage on his work and life was enormous. And despite Baldwin's often-strained attempt to write critically acclaimed novels, it was his capacity to use a moral rhetoric imbued with the rhythms and themes of black holiness culture that will continue to be compelling decades hence even as his largely failed novelistic ventures continue to fade from view. When Gore Vidal appeared on C-SPAN recently for an interview and call-in program, he was asked to assess the work of Baldwin, who was an acquaintance of his during the sixties. Late in the three-hour program, Vidal suggested that most of the novels seemed dated today but that his "sermons" still held up quite well. By sermons Vidal clearly was pointing to Baldwin's essays spiked with the language of passionate and explicit moral commitment over against his sexy Parisian and New York novels, where the hip posture has failed to wear well over time. Indeed, with the exceptions of *Go Tell It* and perhaps *Giovanni's Room*, I believe it is the essays brimming with the heat of his moral rhetoric that will remain compelling and important decades from now.

Although most of his later novelistic efforts were unwieldy affairs, they have been invaluable resources for my investigation of Baldwin's connection with black holiness culture. Baldwin's novels force us to see how complicated his relationship with Christianity truly was. With his novels in view it is impossible to simplify Baldwin's conflicted connection with religion into a simple piety. Where most critics largely ignored Baldwin's peculiar relationship with Christianity, those who had more religiously anchored concerns all too often depicted Baldwin as a "closeted" Christian who embraced Christian sensibilities while eschewing any organic connection to the institutional, organized church. These earlier attempts to describe Baldwin's religious posture fail to bring the sophisticated method and interpretation that Baldwin's complicated life and struggles with love and sex, self-loathing, and exilic displacement demand.

My beloved wife asked me quite pointedly one day, supposedly in jest, whether I made any real distinction in my ongoing project between Baldwin's conception of reality and my own. Beneath this good-natured joshing that we often share in, she was cautioning me not to read too much of myself and my own preoccupations and various neuroses into the life and thought of Jimmy

Baldwin. Jimmy and I, in fact, are quite different. Of course, I have often felt strongly alienated from my own religious upbringing. But my estrangement is much more abstract and detached than Baldwin's ever was. Jimmy's alienation was more dynamic than mine partly because he was more honest about how much personal hurt there really was beneath his expressions of doubt and disappointment with the Christian god. As a black bisexual man, Jimmy's estrangement from holiness culture was more embodied—that is, more in the body—than my grievances against the righteous are. In all of his complaints, Jimmy's human hurt and vulnerability are always clear. His intense struggle with a religious upbringing that so often betrayed him startle me still. Indeed, his struggle with a faith so vibrant with possibility highlight the sharp contradictions of a religious heritage we both share and humbles me as I consider my own petty struggles with the faith of my youth and my present. Baldwin's willingness to directly engage the evangelical impulses within black religion not only prefigured the final decline of Afro-Protestantism as a principal force in black life in North America, but also helped to open the literary space for authors like Toni Morrison and Octavia Butler to embrace new religious worlds.

Even though Baldwin might have helped open the door for religious visions beyond Afro-Protestantism, he will be forever connected to the black holiness culture. He was willing to leave God's house for the art, drink, and risks of a life fully lived, but he retained notions of redemptive suffering even after Martin King's death. Baldwin throughout his career would both employ and disdain the language of judgment that animates evangelicalism and evangelicalism itself. Witnessing this paradoxical relationship Baldwin maintained with black holiness culture, I see myself very much in the shoes of old Meridian, who stands before God in wonder, utter bewilderment, and anger. In *Blues for Mister Charlie*, Meridian sees the New World as a land where he and his kin have lived out their lives with musical joy and the pain of displacement and exile. In examining Baldwin's work we see Christianity in the same way—within its confines, black people have demonstrated their humanity and lived lives of joy and passion and of loss and pain. From its inception within the framework of Christianity, black religion in the United States has been a compromised endeavor. While it has often been the site of group identity and the place where many found a measure of rest for a time filled with struggle, Christianity has at times contributed to the severe disfigurement of black people where many believed the lies about how "ugly" it was to be black and wondered aloud whether our sufferings were divinely intended. I only wish we could see and name these contradictions more freely and accept how compromised this faith is that our ancestors have left us. We would do this not so we could leave old ways behind but so we could achieve the freedom we can within the symbolic universe we have inherited. I can only hope this work will contribute to this effort.

Randall Kenan in his most recent book of the black experience in the United States recounts a strained conversation he had at a café in New York City with an Ethiopian princess who was married to a native black North Carolinian. "You North American blacks, you make me so angry," Kenan remembers his friend saying. "You set yourselves off from the rest of the Diaspora. As if your experiences were somehow *better.*" However defensive Kenan may have been, his response is instructive:

> I don't think American black people think they are any better than Africans or West Indians, but we do recognize that our experience has been markedly different. . . . [W]e've become a part of this country in a way that no other black group has become a part of their country. I mean we made this country. We still do . . . . [W]e've contributed to every aspect of American life, scientifically, legislatively, militarily, artistically . . . . Hell, we are America. We have more claim to this country than anyone other than the Native Americans . . . [H]ow can we ignore our blood-and-sweat connection to this land?[1]

Many, including Baldwin, hold this same view that black people in the United States have a special, unique place in American society unknown to any other group of black people in any other land. But what are we to make of this close identification of black people to the land to which they have been exiled? Even though black people may be what Baldwin calls a bastard people, their closeness to the wayward parent of a West that still refuses to claim its black kin is no great gift, however real this closeness may be. It gives no special status and ability to lead the larger African community throughout a Diaspora that finds itself to be much more distant, though less compromised, from contradictions of identity than their kin found within the United States. Precisely because this fundamental displacement has occurred perhaps more completely than anywhere else in the African Diaspora, this closeness to what makes America America bespeaks of a tragedy at least as much as it hints at promise and hope. To be close to American identity, despite (and perhaps because of) its riches, power, and even freedoms, is to be confronted face to face to the terrible attractiveness of a white social identity—a social identity that flounders before its pretensions—its false and forced innocence.

And it is this tragic position that ultimately shapes black religion in the United States and defines its limits, even as it has become the anchor and bulwark of black identity from comprised enslaved beginnings until today's complicated realities. For me, then, Baldwin demonstrates this tragic undercurrent beneath the posture, rhythms, expressiveness, and humanity of black religion. My work here was meant to show how the limitations of the black holiness culture Baldwin experienced might illuminate the ways black people have related to Christianity in the creation of Afro-Protestantism and more broadly to American culture and society. These "sermons" Vidal mentioned on C-SPAN surely speak to the psychosexual dimensions of white supremacy more profoundly than anything else. And his much-derided fiction encapsulates a complicated vision where Christian conversion bodily enacts at the center of black holiness culture the fundamental displacement, sexual and otherwise, of black exilic experience in the midst of a hostile white Christian culture. But what Baldwin's work demonstrates most clearly is that black religion, like the blues, represents the tragic in an American culture that largely through its forced innocence and disengagement avoids or denies the tough reality of death and racial injustice.

What initially attracts Baldwin to black holiness culture is not tragedy, however, but the performative aspects of black people's religious practice. I know for myself that the music and the drama of black religion—of conversion-brokered religion—can have quite a grip on the human personality. Its hold can be so firm that even Baldwin, who found black institutional Christianity more compromised than I, found within its cultural expressions a posture of humanity, if not always one of overt resistance, that has enacted an admirable measure of strength, community, and identity. As Baldwin said, assuring us all the while that he was not joking but serious. "I am working," he said, "toward the New Jerusalem." And even as Derrick Bell warns of the "permanence of racism" and how white supremacy is so ingrained in society that it is intrinsic to the American identity, we have no other choice but to seek this "new Jerusalem" of justice wherever we can find it. Baldwin believed it could be achieved with love. And even though I am not as sanguine as Baldwin seems to have been of such a project, perhaps Baldwin was right. Maybe we really can be "better than we are."[2]

Notes

Preface

1. James Baldwin, *No Name in the Street* (New York: Dial Press, 1972), 5.

2. James Baldwin, *The Fire Next Time* (1963; reprint, New York: Dell, 1964), 59.

3. Cecil Cone, *The Identity Crisis in Black Theology* (Nashville: African Methodist Episcopal Church, 1975).

4. Theophus Smith, *Conjuring Culture: Biblical Formations of Black America* (New York: Oxford Univ. Press, 1994), ix.

5. Robert E. Hood, *Begrimed and Black: Christian Traditions on Blacks and Blackness* (Minneapolis: Fortress Press, 1994); Delores Williams, *Sisters of the Wilderness* (Maryknoll, N.Y.: Orbis Books, 1993).

6. Ann Taves, *Fits, Trances, and Visions: Experiencing Religion and Explaining Experience from Wesley to James* (Princeton, N.J.: Princeton Univ. Press, 1999), 353.

7. For a hint of these criticisms of Smith, see Dwight Hopkins's review of *Conjuring Culture*, by Theophus Smith, *Journal of Religion* (July 1995): 435–36; and Jennifer Wojcikowski, review of *Conjuring Culture*, by Theophus Smith, *Church History* (Dec. 1999): 1064–65.

Chapter 1

1. David Leeming, *James Baldwin: A Biography* (New York: Henry Holt and Co., 1994), 383.

2. "Black Girl Shouting," quoted in James Campbell, *Talking at the Gates: A Life of James Baldwin* (New York: Viking, 1991), 16.

3. Baldwin, *The Fire*, 44.

4. James Baldwin, *The Devil Finds Work: An Essay* (1976; reprint, New York: Random House, 2000), 33.

5. James Baldwin, "Introduction: The Price of the Ticket," in *The Price of the Ticket: Collected Nonfiction, 1948–1985* (New York: Knopf, 1985), xvi.

6. See, for example, Victor Turner, *From Ritual to Theatre: The Human Seriousness of Play* (New York: Performing Arts Journal Publications, 1982).

7. Baldwin, *The Devil Finds Work*, 29.

8. James Baldwin, *The Amen Corner* (New York: Dial Press, 1968), xvi.

9. Leeming, *James Baldwin*, 17.

10. Baldwin, *The Devil Finds Work*, 30.

11. Ibid., 35.

12. Fern Marja Eckman, *The Furious Passage of James Baldwin* (London: Michael Joseph, 1966), 127; Baldwin, *The Devil Finds Work*, 31.

13. Baldwin, *The Devil Finds Work*, 31.

14. James Baldwin was born James Jones to the then unwed Berdis Jones in Harlem Hospital in 1924 and had no biological connection with David Baldwin, the man who married his mother in 1927. I will refer to his stepfather as his father, just as Baldwin usually did, unless James Baldwin's status as a child born outside of wedlock is pertinent and under discussion.

15. Baldwin, *Fire*, 44–45; for a description of Mother Horn's church based on photographs taken during the late 1940s by Baldwin friend and collaborator Theodore Pelatowski, see Campbell, *Talking at the Gates*, 36.

16. For a brief, biographical essay on Horn, along with a small selection of her sermons where she defends her right to preach, see Bettye Collier-Thomas, ed., *Daughters of Thunder: Black Women Preachers and Their Sermons, 1850–1979* (San Francisco: Jossey-Bass Publishers, 1998), 173–93. For Horn's place in the Harlem community and religious life, see Cheryl Lynn Greenberg, *"Or Does It Explode?" Black Harlem in the Great Depression* (New York: Oxford Univ. Press, 1991), 59, and Campbell, *Talking at the Gates*, 36.

17. Baldwin, *Fire*, 43–44.

18. Ibid., 55.

19. Ibid.

20. James Baldwin, *Go Tell It on the Mountain* (1952; reprint, New York: Laurel, 1985), 120–21.

21. Baldwin, *Fire*, 51.

22. James Baldwin interview with Studs Terkel in Fred L. Standley and Louis H. Pratt, eds., *Conversations with James Baldwin* (Jackson: Univ. of Press of Mississippi, 1989), 23.

23. Baldwin, *Go Tell It*, 34.

24. James Baldwin, "A Fly in Buttermilk," in *Nobody Knows My Name* (New York: Dell, 1961), 76.

25. James Baldwin, "Everybody's Protest Novel," in *Notes of a Native Son* (Boston: Beacon Press, 1955), 17.

26. Baldwin, *Fire*, 49.

27. In his biography, David Leeming, who was one of several close friends with Baldwin in his closing days, recalls a conversation about religion a week before his death. "During the night he [Baldwin] wanted to talk about religion," Leeming writes. "He realized that the church's role in his life had been significant, especially with respect to what he called his 'inner vocabulary.' As for the larger questions, he did not 'believe' in God, but he felt—especially when he was alone—that there was 'something out there.'" See Leeming, *James Baldwin*, 384.

28. Leeming, *James Baldwin*, 99.

29. James Baldwin and Margaret Mead, *A Rap on Race* (New York: Dell, 1971), 83.

30. Baldwin, *The Devil Finds Work*, 125.

31. Michael Lynch, "A Glimpse of the Hidden God: Dialectical Vision in Baldwin's *Go Tell It on the Mountain*" in *New Essays on Go Tell It on the Mountain*, ed. Trudier Harris (New York: Cambridge Univ. Press, 1995), 34.

32. Baldwin, "Introduction," xix.

33. James Baldwin, "White Racism or World Community?" in *The Price of the Ticket*, 440.

34. Baldwin, "White Racism or World Community?" 436.

35. Barbara K. Olson, "Come-to-Jesus Stuff" in James Baldwin's *Go Tell It on the Mountain* and *The Amen Corner*," *African American Review* 31 (summer 1997): 299.

36. Baldwin, *Go Tell It*, 221.

37. Olson, "Come-to-Jesus Stuff," 299.

38. Olson, "Come-to-Jesus Stuff," 299.

39. Baldwin, *The Amen Corner*, xvi.

40. Critic Carlton Molette quoted in Olson, "Come-to-Jesus Stuff," 298.

41. Baldwin, *The Amen Corner*, xvi.

42. Nathan A. Scott Jr., "Judgement Marked by a Cellar: The American Negro Writer and the Dialectic of Despair," in *The Shapeless God*, ed. Harry J. Monney Jr. and Thomas F. Staley (Pittsburgh: Univ. of Pittsburgh Press, 1968), 163.

43. See, for example, Shirley S. Allen, "Religious Symbolism and Psychic Reality in Baldwin's *Go Tell It on the Mountain*," *CLA Journal* 19 (1975): 173–99; Edward Margolies, *Native Sons: A Critical Study of Twentieth-Century Negro American Authors* (New York: Lippincott, 1968). A contemporary approach that mirrors these other ones is Lynch, "A Glimpse of a Hidden God."

44. Baldwin and Mead, *A Rap on Race*, 89.

45. James Baldwin interview with John Hall, in Standley and Pratt, *Conversations with James Baldwin,* 106.

46. See, for example, William R. Jones, *Is God a White Racist?* (Garden City, N.Y.: Anchor Press/Doubleday, 1973).

47. Baldwin, "White Racism or World Community?" 441.

48. See, for example, feminist Rosemary Ruether's seminal work, *Sexism and God-Talk: Toward a Feminist Theology* (Boston: Beacon Press, 1983), 116–38.

49. Examples of this perspective abound. See Michel Fabre, "Fathers and Sons in James Baldwin's *Go Tell It on the Mountain,*" in *James Baldwin: A Collection of Critical Essays,* ed. Kenneth Kinnamon (Englewood Cliff, N.J.: Prentice-Hall, 1974); Nagueyalti Warren, "The Substance of Things Hoped For: Faith in *Go Tell It on the Mountain,*" *Obsidian II 7* (spring–summer 1992): 19–32.

50. Patricia Lorine Schnapp, "The Liberation Theology of James Baldwin," (Ph.D. diss., Bowling Green State Univ., 1987), 19.

51. As Lawrence Van Heusen writes: "Baldwin affirms the experience of religion and reflects the difficulty of embodying that experience in any single word. For it is the religious experience, a *revelation,* deep and nearly inarticulable, which Baldwin consistently pursues in his writing." See Van Heusen's "The Embodiment of Religious Meaning in the Works of James Baldwin" (D.A. diss., State Univ. of New York at Albany, 1980), 2.

52. Baldwin, "White Racism or World Community?" 435.

53. For a history of the early development of the black Holiness-Pentecostal movement and its origins in the largely rural Mississippi Delta, see David Daniels III, "The Cultural Renewal of Slave Religion: Charles Price Jones and the Emergence of the Holiness Movement in Mississippi" (Ph.D. diss., Union Theological Seminary, 1992); John Giggie, "God's Long Journey: African Americans, Religion, and History in the Mississippi Delta, 1875–1915" (Ph.D. diss., Princeton Univ., 1997), 201. Concerning this movement's transition to an urban context parallel with the emergence of the Great Migration, see C. Eric Lincoln and Lawrence H. Mamiya, *The Black Church in the African American Experience* (Durham: Duke Univ. Press, 1990), 82, 125.

54. Baldwin, *Go Tell It,* 15–16.

55. Ibid., 16–17.

Chapter 2

1. See Clayborne Carson, "Martin Luther King, Jr., and the African-American Social Gospel," in *African-American Christianity: Essays in History,* ed. Paul E. Johnson (Berkeley: Univ. of California Press, 1994), 159–77, for the

example of African Methodist Episcopal (AME) bishop Daniel Payne, who during the 1870s and 1880s rejected the kinetic religious expression of various prayer "bands" and insisted that they "desist and . . . sit down and sing in a rational manner" and avoid the "disgraceful," "heathenish way" of worship. A young leader of one of the "bands" still continued to insist on "the singing and clapping ring" because, in his words, "Sinners won't get converted unless there is a ring." See Daniel Alexander Payne, *Recollections of Seventy Years* (1886; New York: Arno Press and New York Times, 1969), 253–55.

2. See Paul Harvey, "'Those Untutored Masses': The Campaign for Respectability among White and Black Evangelicals in the American South, 1870–1930," *Journal of Religious History* 21, no. 3 (Oct. 1997): 302–17; Evelyn Brooks Higginbotham, *Righteous Discontent: The Women's Movement in the Black Baptist Church, 1880–1920* (Cambridge, Mass.: Harvard Univ. Press, 1993); Christine Leigh Heyrman, *Southern Cross: The Beginnings of the Bible Belt* (New York: Knopf, 1997).

3. The black Holiness-Pentecostal movement that emerged in the beginning of the twentieth century, which stressed conversion, dance, and the ecstatic experience, most exemplifies the evangelical aspects of black religion. Of course, the more mainstream and established Baptist and Methodist communions also exhibit this impulse, particularly in the call-and-response rhythms of preaching and the mournful, metered music so prevalent during the midweek evening prayer meetings and the devotional, a testimony period that often precedes Sunday morning worship. See Walter F. Pitts's exemplary examination of ritual in rural Texas Baptist churches in his *Old Ship of Zion: The Afro-Baptist Ritual in the African Diaspora* (New York: Oxford Univ. Press, 1993); cf. Morton Marks, "Uncovering Ritual Structures in Afro-American Music," in *Religious Movements in Contemporary America*, ed. Irving Zaretsky and Mark Leone (Princeton, N.J.: Princeton Univ. Press, 1974).

4. Baldwin, *The Fire*, 47.

5. James Baldwin, *The Evidence of Things Not Seen* (New York: Henry Holt and Co., 1985), 83.

6. Charles Stearn, *Narrative of Henry Box Brown* (Boston: Brown and Stearns, 1849), 17–18.

7. See Samuel Miller Lawton, "The Religious Life of South Carolina Coastal and Sea Island Negroes" (Ph.D. diss., George Peabody College for Teachers, 1939), 143–44, quoted in Albert Raboteau, *Slave Religion: The "Invisible Institutions" in the Antebellum South* (New York: Oxford Univ. Press, 1978), 73, and Margaret Washington Creel, *"A Peculiar People": Slave Religion and Community-Culture among the Gullahs* (New York: New York Univ. Press, 1988),

287; Joseph M. Murphy, *Working the Spirit: Ceremonies of the African Diaspora* (Boston: Beacon Press, 1994), 78.

8. James Baldwin interview with Jewell Handy Gresham, in Standley and Pratt, *Conversations with James Baldwin*, 163.

9. Baldwin, *Go Tell It*, 199. The "cloud of witnesses" refers to Heb. 12:1, as rendered in the cadences of the King James Version of the Bible.

10. Thomas A. Burns and J. Stephen Smith, "The Symbolism of Becoming in the Sunday Service of an Urban Black Holiness Church," *Anthropological Quarterly* 51, no. 3 (July 1978).

11. Baldwin, *Go Tell It*, 145.

12. Ibid., 188–89.

13. Baldwin, *The Fire*, 27.

14. Ibid., 27–29.

15. Baldwin, *Go Tell It*, 11.

16. See Taves, *Fits, Trances, and Visions*, 76–117; see also Ann Taves, "Knowing through the Body: Dissociative Religious Experience in the African-American and British-American Methodist Traditions," *Journal of Religion* 73, no. 2 (Apr. 1993): 200–222, and Mechal Sobel, *Trabelin' On: The Slave Journey to an Afro-Baptist Faith* (Westport, Conn.: Greenwood Press, 1979), 139–80.

17. William C. Johnson, "'To Dance in the Ring of All Creation': Camp Meeting Revivalism and the Color Line, 1799–1825" (Ph.D. diss., Univ. of California at Riverside, 1997), 173–74.

18. Quoted in Johnson, "To Dance in a Ring of All Creation," 144.

19. Ibid.

20. Baldwin, *Go Tell It*, 136–37.

21. Baldwin, "Introduction," xviii.

22. Baldwin, *Go Tell It*, 96.

23. Trudier Harris, *Black Women in the Fiction of James Baldwin* (Knoxville: Univ. of Tennessee Press, 1985), 46.

24. Baldwin, *Go Tell It*, 94.

25. Ibid., 131.

26. James Baldwin, *If Beale Street Could Talk* (New York: Dial Press, 1974), 22.

27. This turn of phrase that describes whiteness as a form of apostasy without self-consciousness comes from Willie Earl Walker's description of Gabriel in his dissertation. Later I will link Baldwin's initial characterization of Gabriel to his evolving understanding of the nature and character of white social identity. See Willie Earl Walker III, "Prophetic Articulations: James Baldwin and the Racial Formation of the United States" (Ph.D. diss., Princeton Univ., 1999), 53.

28. The supposed Hamitic curse Baldwin references here and elsewhere is connected to how Genesis 9 and 10 have been interpreted to legitimatize the naturalness of the enslavement of African peoples. After the mythical flood that destroys most of the earth and its inhabitants, Ham sees his drunken father, Noah, naked even as the other sons cover their father without gazing on him. When he awakens sober and angry, Noah curses Canaan, Ham's son, and says that he and his progeny will be the "servant of servants." Given that Jewish midrash and various Christian scholars during the medieval period began to associate Ham and Canaanites with Africans, it is not surprising that opportunistic white planters eager to give their brutal exploitation of enslaved Africans biblical sanction invoked this "Hamitic curse" with great frequency to support slavery. See Winthrop Jordan's, *White over Black: American Attitudes toward the Negro, 1550–1812* (Baltimore: Penguin Books, 1968), 17–20, 35–37, 41–43, 158, 245–46, and Hood, *Begrimed and Black*, 155–80.

29. Baldwin, *The Fire*, 59.

30. Eli Shephard, "Certain Beliefs and Superstitions," in Bruce Jackson, *The Negro and His Folklore* (Austin: Univ. of Texas Press, 1969), 248. I was made aware of this story in a book by Riggins R. Earl where he deploys its meaning in a slightly different way than I suggest here. For his interpretation, see his *Dark Symbols, Obscure Signs: God, Self and Community in the Slave Mind* (Maryknoll, N.Y.: Orbis Books, 1993), 51–52.

31. Earl, *Dark Symbols, Obscure Signs*, 52.

32. Baldwin, "Everybody's Protest Novel," 16.

33. Baldwin, "Notes of a Native Son," in *Notes of a Native Son*, 72–73.

34. For an exploration of how various Christian traditions shaped what would later become the European and American perceptions of blackness, see Robert E. Hood's *Begrimed and Black*.

35. Jordan, *White over Black*, 24, 256, 258. For an exploration of how black religious expression, whatever its stripe, has long been associated with the demonic, see also Joseph M. Murphy, "Black Religion and 'Black Magic': Prejudice and Projection in Images of African-Derived Religions," *Religion* (1990): 20, 323–37.

36. Baldwin, *Go Tell It*, 27.

37. Ibid., 197, 199.

38. Baldwin, *The Devil Finds Work*, 6–7.

39. James Baldwin interview with Eve Auchincloss and Nancy Lynch, in Standley and Pratt, *Conversations with James Baldwin*, 78–79.

40. Baldwin, "Introduction," xii.

41. For an analysis of how Baldwin perceived the Christian god as a wayward primal father who acts as, and in many ways replaces, his stepfather, David Baldwin, see Sondra O'Neale, "Fathers, Gods, and Religion: Perceptions of Christianity and Ethnic Faith in James Baldwin," in *Critical Essays on James Baldwin*, ed. Fred Standley and Nancy V. Burt (Boston: G. K. Hall, 1988). O'Neale's article also anticipates many of the themes of this present work. See also Michel Fabre, "Fathers and Sons in James Baldwin's *Go Tell It on the Mountain*," in *James Baldwin: A Collection of Critical Essays*, ed. Kenneth Kinnamon (Englewood Cliffs, N.J.: Prentice-Hall, 1974).

42. Baldwin interview with Terkel, in Standley and Pratt, *Conversations with James Baldwin*, 5.

43. Baldwin, *Blues for Mister Charlie*, 56.

44. Ibid.

45. Ibid.

46. See Albert J. Raboteau, "The Conversion Experience," in his collection of essays, *A Fire in the Bones: Reflections on African-American History* (Boston: Beacon Press, 1995), 152–65. Also see Paul Radin, "Status, Fantasy, and the Christian Dogma," in *God Struck Me Dead: Voices of Ex-Slaves*, ed. Clifton H. Johnson (1969; reprint, Cleveland: Pilgrim Press, 1993), viii.

47. James Baldwin interview with Kalamu ya Salaam, in Standley and Pratt, *Conversations with James Baldwin*, 182.

48. Baldwin, *Go Tell It*, 20–21.

49. Ibid., 194.

50. Ibid., 198.

51. James Baldwin, "The Discovery of What It Means to Be an American," in *The Price of the Ticket*, 171.

52. Baldwin, *Go Tell It*, 22.

53. This passage from Isa. 6:5 is quoted at the beginning of part 3, entitled "The Threshing Floor," in Baldwin, *Go Tell It*, 191.

54. Remembering Ayer's influence on him in a 1963 interview, Baldwin tells the famous psychologist Kenneth Clark: "[A]t the point I was going to P.S. 24 the only Negro school principal as far as I know in the entire history of New York was a principal named Mrs. Ayer, and she liked me. In a way I guess she proved to me that I didn't have to be entirely defined by my circumstances." See the Baldwin interview with Clark, in Standley and Pratt, *Conversations with James Baldwin*, 40. See also Eckman, *The Furious Passage*, 42–43.

55. Baldwin, *Go Tell It*, 20.

56. Baldwin, *The Amen Corner*, 62.

57. Baldwin, "Everybody's Protest Novel," 15.

58. James Baldwin, "Many Thousands Gone," in *Notes of a Native Son,* 22–23.

59. James Baldwin, "Autobiographical Notes," in *Notes of a Native Son,* 4.

60. Baldwin, "Everybody's Protest Novel," 16.

61. W. E. B. Du Bois, *The Souls of Black Folk* (New York: First Vintage Books/Library of America Edition, 1990), 9.

62. For the connections between Du Bois's *The Souls of Black Folk* and Baldwin's *Notes of a Native* Son, see Lauren Rusk, "Selfhood and Strategy in *Notes a Native Son,*" in *James Baldwin Now,* ed. Dwight A. McBride (New York: New York Univ. Press, 1999), 360–92.

63. Baldwin, "Everybody's Protest Novel," 16.

64. James Baldwin with Nikki Giovanni, *A Dialogue* (Philadelphia: J. B. Lippincott, 1973), 17.

65. William E. B. Du Bois, *Darkwater: Voices from within the Veil* (New York: Harcourt, Brace, and Howe, 1920), 27.

66. Baldwin, *Beale Street,* 28.

Chapter 3

1. Baldwin, "World Racism or World Community?" in *Price of the Ticket,* 435.

2. James, *No Name,* 5.

3. Baldwin, *Go Tell It,* 137.

4. Ibid., 138.

5. Baldwin, "Notes of a Native Son," 72, 74, 86.

6. Baldwin, *Go Tell It,* 81.

7. James Baldwin, *Tell Me How Long the Train's Been Gone* (New York: Dell, 1968), 162.

8. Baldwin, *The Fire,* 45.

9. James Baldwin's "Peace on Earth," quoted in Campbell, *Talking at the Gates,* 18.

10. For the complete text of James Baldwin's "Incident in London," which first appeared in the Spring of 1941 in the pages of *Magpie,* a publication of De Witt Clinton High School of the Bronx, New York, see Eckman, *The Furious Passage,* 83.

11. Eckman, *The Furious Passage,* 73.

12. "Jimmy was even more devout than I was," Arthur Moore tells an early Baldwin biographer. "He went to church more and more. We'd often go together, several nights a week, arriving about eight and coming home at eleven

or twelve. The Pentecostal faith believes you must be in the world, but not of the world. You mustn't smoke or dance or go to the movies. Jimmy and I didn't swear, didn't smoke, didn't go to the movies, didn't dance." See Eckman, *The Furious Passage*, 74.

13. Baldwin, *The Fire*, 46.

14. James Baldwin, "The Outing," in *Going to Meet the Man* (1965; reprint, New York: Laurel, 1988), 29.

15. Baldwin, *Go Tell It*, 84.

16. Ibid., 193.

17. Baldwin, *The Fire*, 44–47.

18. Baldwin, *The Devil Finds Work*, 119.

19. Baldwin, *The Fire*, 45.

20. Ibid., 46.

21. Ibid., 56.

22. Trudier Harris, introduction to *New Essays on* Go Tell It on the Mountain, 21.

23. Ernest A. Champion, *Mr. Baldwin, I Presume: James Baldwin-Chinua Achebe, a Meeting of the Minds* (Lanham, Md.: Univ. Press of America, 1995), 139.

24. Nella Larsen, *Quicksand and Passing*, ed. Deborah E. McDowell (New Brunswick, N.J.: Rutgers Univ. Press, 1986), 113.

25. Ibid., 114.

26. Ibid., 130, 133.

27. David Leeming, Baldwin's biographer, sees Leo as perhaps the character based most transparently on James Baldwin's life and thinking since his first novel, *Go Tell It*. If so, this novel, unlike his first effort, was not the better for it. See Leeming, *James Baldwin*, 278.

28. Baldwin, *Tell Me How Long*, 75–76.

29. Donald B. Gibson, "James Baldwin: The Political Anatomy of Space," in *James Baldwin: A Critical Evaluation*, ed. Therman B. O'Daniel (Washington: Howard Univ. Press, 1977), 15.

30. Larsen, *Quicksand*, 130.

31. Baldwin, *The Fire*, 134.

32. James Baldwin, "The Harlem Ghetto," in *Notes of a Native Son*, 55.

33. Baldwin, *The Fire*, 134.

34. Ibid., 124.

35. James Baldwin's conversation with Niebuhr, "Meaning of the Birmingham Tragedy," Reinhold Niebuhr Audio Tape Collection, Union Theological Seminary in Virginia, Tape #61; Baldwin quoted in Taylor Branch, *Parting the Waters: America in the King Years, 1954–1963* (New York: Simon and Schuster,

1988), 895. For more information about the "missing face of Christ" and the Birmingham bombing, see Frank Sikora, *Until Justice Rolls Down: The Birmingham Church Bombing Case* (Tuscaloosa: Univ. of Alabama Press, 1991), 1–37.

36. Baldwin quoted in Champion, *Mr. Baldwin, I Presume*, 27.

37. Willie Earl Walker III, "Prophetic Articulations: James Baldwin and the Racial Formation of the United States" (Ph.D. diss., Princeton Univ., 1999), 109.

38. James Baldwin, "Notes for a Hypothetical Novel," in *Nobody Knows My Name* (New York: Dell, 1961), 126.

39. D. Quentin Miller, introduction to *Re-Viewing James Baldwin: Things Not Seen*, ed. D. Quentin Miller (Philadelphia: Temple Univ. Press, 2000), 3.

40. Michael F. Lynch, "Beyond Guilt and Innocence: Redemptive Suffering and Love in Baldwin's *Another Country*," *Obsidian II: Black Literature in Review* 7, no. 1–2 (1992): 1–18; Michael F. Lynch, "Staying Out of the Temple: Baldwin, the African American Church, and *The Amen Corner*," in *Re-viewing James Baldwin*, ed. D. Quentin Miller, 33–71. For a parallel analysis on the redemptive power of suffering, see Harris, *Black Women in the Fiction of James Baldwin*, 81.

41. Lynch, "Beyond Guilt and Innocence," 4.

42. Baldwin, "Autobiographical Notes," 2.

43. Baldwin, *The Amen Corner*, 41–42.

44. Baldwin, *Tell Me How Long*, 76.

45. I use the word *manhood* quite deliberately here. As inclusive as Baldwin's notion of love is, it is not clear to me that his understanding of white supremacy and suffering go much beyond his conception of racism as injured manhood. Even as Baldwin attempts to redefine the bounds of masculinity in a radical fashion, the deeply harmful exclusion of women from his analysis of white supremacy will only become clearer as we examine Baldwin's overall work.

46. James Baldwin, *Another Country* (New York: Dial Press, 1962), 329.

47. Baldwin, *Tell Me How Long*, 76.

48. James Baldwin, "The Uses of the Blues: How a Uniquely American Art Form Relates to the Negro's Fight for His Rights," *Playboy*, Jan. 1964, 131.

49. Baldwin, *No Name*, 9.

50. James Baldwin interview with John Hall, in Standley and Pratt, *Conversations with James Baldwin*, 102–3.

51. Baldwin, *No Name*, 10.

52. Ibid., 194.

53. Ibid., 54.

54. Ibid., 54.

55. Ibid., 9–10.

56. Baldwin, *Go Tell It*, 14.

57. Saadi A. Simawe, "What Is in a Sound? The Metaphysics and Politics of Music in *The Amen Corner*," in *Re-Viewing James Baldwin: Things Not Seen*, ed. D. Quentin Miller (Philadelphia: Temple Univ. Press, 2000), 29. Simawe's interpretation in this article has greatly influenced my own for much of the discussion that follows.

58. Baldwin, *The Amen Corner*, 5–6.

59. James Baldwin, *Just Above My Head* (New York: Dial Press, 1979), 16.

60. Baldwin, *The Amen Corner*, 44.

61. John M. Reilly, "Sonny's Blues: James Baldwin's Image of Black Community," in *James Baldwin: A Collection of Critical Essays*, ed. Kenneth Kinnamon (Englewood Cliffs, N.J.: Prentice Hall, 1974), 140.

62. James Baldwin, "Sonny's Blues," in *Going to Meet the Man*, 111, 114.

63. Ibid., 111–12.

64. Ibid., 119.

65. Daniel E. Walker, "Pleading the Blood: Storefront Pentecostalism in James Baldwin's 'Sonny's Blues,'" *CLA Journal* 43, no. 2 (Dec. 1999): 203.

66. James Baldwin with Nikki Giovanni, *A Dialogue* (Philadelphia: J. B. Lippincott, 1973), 80.

67. Baldwin, "Sonny's Blues," 120.

68. Ibid., 122.

Chapter 4

1. Baldwin with Giovanni, *A Dialogue*, 38.

2. Baldwin, "World Racism or World Community?" 441.

3. Baldwin with Giovanni, *A Dialogue*, 38.

4. James Baldwin, *Blues for Mister Charlie* (New York: Dial Press, 1964), 125.

5. Ibid., 125.

6. Baldwin with Giovanni, *A Dialogue*, 37.

7. Baldwin, *Another Country*, 305.

8. Baldwin with Giovanni, *A Dialogue*, 40.

9. James Baldwin, "Here Be Dragons," in *The Price of the Ticket*, 678.

10. Baldwin, *The Fire*, 128.

11. Baldwin, *Another Country*, 180.

12. James Baldwin and Colin MacInnes interview with James Mossman, in Standley and Pratt, *Conversations with James Baldwin*, 48.

13. Baldwin, *The Fire*, 124.

14. Baldwin, *The Amen Corner,* 88.

15. Ibid.

16. Baldwin, *Just Above My Head,* 24.

17. Baldwin, *Another Country,* 173–74.

18. Ibid., 176.

19. Baldwin, *Beale Street,* 17–18.

20. Ibid., 42.

21. Trudier Harris, "The Eye as Weapon in *If Beale Street Could Talk,*" *MELUS* 5, no. 3 (1978): 62–64.

22. Baldwin, *Beale Street,* 143.

23. James Baldwin, "Every Good-Bye Ain't Gone," in *The Price of the Ticket,* 647.

24. Baldwin, *The Devil Finds Work,* 125.

25. Baldwin, *Another Country,* 170.

26. Kevin Ohi, "'I'm Not the Boy You Want': Sexuality, Race, and Thwarted Revelation in Baldwin's *Another Country,*" *African American Review* 33, no. 2 (spring 1999): 261–81.

27. The clearest example of this is Lawrence Van Heusen's dissertation, "The Embodiment of Religious Meaning in the Works of James Baldwin." Of course Van Heusen's presentation does not focus enough on the ambiguities inherent in many of Baldwin's attempts to grasp revelation as a central metaphor for human experience. Ohi, in his recent article, on the other hand, does not connect Baldwin's anguished vision of sexual expression as revelatory with his past history in holiness church culture.

28. Baldwin, *Another Country,* 147.

29. Baldwin, *Beale Street,* 52.

30. William A. Cohen, "Liberalism, Libido, Liberation: Baldwin's *Another Country,*" *Genders* 12 (winter 1991): 17; for similar perspectives, see James A. Dievler, "Sexual Exiles: James Baldwin and *Another Country,*" in McBride, *James Baldwin Now,* 161–83.

31. James Baldwin interview with Richard Goldstein in *James Baldwin: The Legacy,* ed. Quincy Troupe (New York: Simon & Schuster, 1989), 174. Emphasis mine.

32. See again the Baldwin interview with Goldstein in Troupe, *James Baldwin,* 180, where Baldwin says: "I think white gay people feel cheated because they were born, in principle, into a society in which they were supposed to be safe. The anomaly of their sexuality puts them in danger, unexpectedly. Their reaction seems to me in direct proportion to the sense of feeling cheated of the advantages which accrue to white people in a white society.

There's an element, it has always seemed to me, of bewilderment and complaint. Now that may sound very harsh, but the gay world as such is no more prepared to accept black people than anywhere else in society. It's a very hermetically sealed world with very unattractive features, including racism."

33. Baldwin, *Just Above My Head*, 48.

34. See, for example, William J. Weatherby's chapter on "Frog Eyes," in his *James Baldwin: Artist on Fire* (New York: D. I. Fine, 1989).

35. Baldwin, *The Evidence of Things Not Seen*, 122.

36. Baldwin, *The Fire*, 57–58.

37. James Baldwin interview with Kalamu ya Salaam, *Conversations with James Baldwin*, 184. The term *life-phobia* comes from the interviewer, who offers the term as Baldwin struggles over whether homophobia totally characterizes "sexual paranoia" in the United States and the Western world.

38. James Baldwin interview with Richard Goldstein in *James Baldwin: The Legacy*, ed. Quincy Troupe (New York: Simon & Schuster, 1989), 178.

39. Following his discussion about the forced sexual availability of black men and women, Baldwin appears to recall his own experience. Baldwin tells Eckman: "And if you're a *black boy* . . . you wouldn't be-*lieve* the holocaust that opens over your head—with all these despicable—*males*—looking for somebody to act out their fantasies on. And it happens in this case—if you're sixteen years old—to be *you*." See Eckman, *Furious Passage*, 32–33.

40. Baldwin interview with Terkel, *Conversations with James Baldwin*, 9.

41. James Baldwin, "History as Nightmare," in *James Baldwin: Collected Essays* (New York: Library of America, 1998), 580.

42. Leeming, *James Baldwin*, 220.

43. Baldwin, *No Name*, 61–62.

44. James Baldwin, "Previous Condition," in *Going to Meet the Man*, 76.

45. Baldwin's manuscript is quoted in Campbell, *Talking at the Gates*, 43.

46. Baldwin, "Here Be Dragons," 686–87.

47. Baldwin, *No Name*, 64.

48. James Darsey, "Baldwin's Cosmopolitan Loneliness," in *James Baldwin Now*, ed. Dwight A. McBride (New York: New York Univ. Press, 1999), 207 n. 106.

49. The most famous of these homophobic attacks was launched by Eldridge Cleaver, who accused gay black men like Baldwin of "bending over and touching their toes for the white man." See Eldridge Cleaver, *Soul on Ice* (New York: McGraw-Hill, 1968), 98–110.

50. Baldwin, *No Name*, 62.

51. Baldwin with Giovanni, *A Dialogue*, 37.

52. Baldwin interview with Goldstein, *James Baldwin: The Legacy,* 177.

53. Baldwin interview with Goldstein, *James Baldwin: The Legacy,* 177.

54. Baldwin, "White Racism or World Community?" 440.

55. James Baldwin, "Preservation of Innocence," in *James Baldwin: Collected Essays,* 594–96.

56. Ibid., 596.

57. Ibid.

58. Baldwin quoted in Eckman, *The Furious Passage,* 32–33.

59. Ibid.

60. Champion, *Baldwin, I Presume,* 137.

61. Baldwin interview with Goldstein in Troupe, *James Baldwin,* 176.

62. Baldwin, *No Name,* 63, 186, 191.

63. Ibid., 186.

64. Ibid., 71–74.

65. Baldwin, *The Fire,* 187.

Chapter 5

1. Charles Ball, *Fifty Years in Chains* (1837; reprint, New York: Dover Publications, 1970), 219–20.

2. Ibid., 221.

3. Clifton H. Johnson and A. P. Watson, eds., *God Struck Me Dead: Religious Conversion Experiences and Autobiographies of American Slaves* (Philadelphia: Pilgrim Press, 1969), 153, 161.

4. Charles Stearn, *Narrative of Henry Box Brown* (Boston: Brown and Stearns, 1849), 18.

5. Baldwin, "The Harlem Ghetto," 54.

6. Baldwin, *Notes of a Native Son,* 54. For the notion of hidden transcript, see James C. Scott, *Domination and the Arts of Resistance: Hidden Transcripts* (New Haven: Yale Univ. Press, 1990). The notion refers to those cultural practices of the marginalized that appear despite the overall appearance of broad societal consent and represent a larger and emergent dissident culture of resistance to sharp material inequality.

7. Baldwin, "Autobiographical Notes," 2.

8. Baldwin, *The Fire,* 140–41. Emphasis mine.

9. Baldwin, "World Racism or World Community?" 441.

10. Baldwin, *The Fire,* 46.

11. Ibid., 72–73.

12. Ibid., 139, 141.

13. Ibid., 64.

14. Baldwin, "Introduction," xviii.

15. Eckman, *The Furious Passage*, 184.

16. See my two sources for this famous meeting between Baldwin and Kennedy in New York City in Leeming, *James Baldwin: A Biography*, 222–24; Taylor Branch, *Parting the Waters: America in the King Years, 1954–63* (New York: Simon and Schuster, 1988), 809–12.

17. James Baldwin interview with Kenneth B. Clark, in Standley and Pratt, *Conversations with James Baldwin*, 41.

18. James Baldwin, "On Being 'White' . . . And Other Lies," in *Black on White: Black Writers on What It Means to Be White*, ed. David R. Roediger (New York: Schocken Books, 1998), 180.

19. Baldwin quoted in Eckman, *The Furious Passage*, 220.

20. Leeming, *James Baldwin*, 48. Emphasis mine.

21. Baldwin friend and biographer David Leeming vividly described these dinner party scenes for me, both in a personal conversation with me in August 1996 and in his biography. See Leeming, *James Baldwin*, 47–48.

22. Leeming, *James Baldwin*, 47–48.

23. Baldwin, *The Fire*, 127–28.

24. Baldwin, *Blues for Mister Charlie*, 58–59.

25. Baldwin, *The Fire*, 129.

26. James H. Cone, *Black Theology and Black Power* (New York: Seabury Press, 1969), 150–51.

27. Baldwin, "Introduction," xx.

28. Baldwin, "On Being 'White,'" 180.

29. See the magisterial work of W. E. B. Du Bois in his *Black Reconstruction* (New York: Harcourt, Brace and Co., 1935). The very presence of this text challenged the dominant interpretation of the Reconstruction period of a generation and set the basic contours still used by the most persuasive contemporary interpretations of that period. See, for example, Eric Foner, *Reconstruction: America's Unfinished Revolution, 1863–1877* (New York: Harper & Row, 1988). For an example of his impact on contemporary whiteness studies, see David R. Roediger, *Wages of Whiteness: Race and the Making of the American Working Class* (London: Verso, 1991). See also Noel Ignatiev, *How the Irish Became White* (New York: Routledge, 1995).

30. Marlon B. Ross, "White Fantasies of Desire: Baldwin and the Racial Identities of Sexuality," in *James Baldwin Now*, ed. Dwight A. McBride (New York: New York Univ. Press, 1999), 25.

31. Du Bois, *Darkwater*, 27.

32. Baldwin, "Here Be Dragons," 690.

33. Baldwin, *The Fire*, 16.

34. W. J. Weatherby describes in his biography of Baldwin how he distrusted psychotherapy. This disregard is quite surprising given the psychologically charged language he uses to reflect how larger societal functions are reflections of inner dysfunction. See Weatherby, *James Baldwin*, 7.

35. Delores S. Williams develops a similar notion about whiteness in her womanist theology. See her *Sisters in the Wilderness: The Challenge of Womanist God-Talk* (Maryknoll, N.Y.: Orbis Books, 1993).

36. Baldwin, *No Name*, 54.

37. For an exploration of the one-drop rule in the history of race in United States, see F. James Davis, *Who Is Black? One Nation's Definition* (University Park: Pennsylvania State Univ. Press, 1991).

38. Baldwin, *Tell Me How Long*, 47.

39. Baldwin, *Blues for Mister Charlie*, 6.

40. For more on how Baldwin used various literary techniques like "self-masking," which he uses to connect with a white audience even as he obscures his own position in the racial hierarchy, see Lauren Rusk's "Selfhood and Strategy in *Notes of a Native Son*," in McBride, *James Baldwin Now*, 360–92.

41. Baldwin, *Blues for Mister Charlie*, 105.

42. Baldwin, "Notes of a Native Son," 74.

43. Ibid., 74–76.

44. Ibid., 76.

45. Ibid., 72–73.

46. Baldwin, "Many Thousands Gone," 19.

47. James Baldwin, *Giovanni's Room* (New York: Dial Press, 1956), 209. My language of imprisonment is meant to echo the title, "The Male Prison," later affixed to an essay published a few short years before *Giovanni's Room*, originally entitled "Gide as Husband and Homosexual."

48. Nathan A. Scott Jr., "Judgment Marked by a Cellar: The American Negro Writer and the Dialectic of Despair," *Denver Quarterly* 2, no. 2 (summer 1967): 27–28.

49. Ross, "White Fantasies of Desire," 25–26.

50. Baldwin, *Giovanni's Room*, 3.

51. William J. Weatherby, *Squaring Off: Mailer vs. Baldwin* (New York: Mason/Charter, 1977), 9.

52. Baldwin, *Giovanni's Room*, 30.

53. Ibid., 30–31.

54. Ibid., 33.

55. Ibid., 77.

56. Ibid., 222–23.

57. "An Interview with James Baldwin on Henry James," interview by David Adams Leeming, *Henry James Review* 8, no. 1 (1986): 49–50, 54–55.

58. "An Interview with James Baldwin on Henry James," 54.

59. Rebecca Aanerud, "Now More Than Ever: James Baldwin and the Critique of White Liberalism," in McBride, *James Baldwin Now*, 64.

60. James Baldwin, "White Man's Guilt," in *The Price of the Ticket*, 410.

61. Baldwin, *Just Above My Head*, 480–81.

62. James Baldwin, "The Black Boy Looks at the White Boy," in *The Price of the Ticket*, 298.

63. Ibid.

64. James Baldwin, "Stranger in the Village," in *Notes of a Native Son*, 148.

65. Baldwin interview with Goldstein in Troupe, *James Baldwin*, 185.

Epilogue

1. Eckman, *Furious Passage*, 22

2. Quoted in Eckman, *Furious Passage*, 15.

3. Baldwin interview with Quincy Troupe in *Conversations with James Baldwin*, 291

4. Baldwin, "Many Thousands Gone," 33.

5. Walker, "Prophetic Articulations," 128.

6. Baldwin, "Stranger in the Village," 147.

7. Baldwin, *Go Tell It*, 137.

8. Baldwin, "The Harlem Ghetto," 56.

9. Baldwin, *Blues for Mister Charlie*, 105.

10. Ibid.

11. Baldwin, "Introduction," xix.

12. James Baldwin interview with Quincy Trope in his *James Baldwin: The Legacy*, 205.

13. Baldwin, *No Name*, 185.

14. James Baldwin and Colin MacInnes interview with James Mossman in *Conversations with James Baldwin*, 50.

15. Cornel West, *Prophesy Deliverance! An Afro-American Revolutionary Christianity* (Philadelphia: Westminster Press, 1982), 84–85.

16. Baldwin interview with Troupe in his *James Baldwin: The Legacy*, 193.

17. Baldwin, "The Uses of the Blues," 241.

18. Donald Gibson, "The Political Anatomy of Space," in *James Baldwin: A Collection of Critical Essays*, ed. Kenneth Kinnamon (Englewood Cliffs, N.J.: Prentice-Hall, 1974), 16.

19. Baldwin, *Tell Me How Long*, 343. In "The Political Anatomy of Space," Gibson quite provocatively begins his own mediation on space and politics in Baldwin's work with this quotation.

20. Baldwin, *The Fire*, 97.

21. Ibid.

22. William Cohen, "Liberalism, Libido, Liberation: Baldwin's *Another Country*," *Genders* 12 (1991): 1–21.

23. James Baldwin and Audre Lorde, "A Revolutionary Hope: Conversation between James Baldwin and Audre Lorde," *Essence*, Dec. 1984, 73.

24. Sondra A. O'Neale, "Fathers, Gods, and Religion: Perceptions of Christianity and Ethnic Faith in James Baldwin," in *Critical Essays on James Baldwin*, ed. Fred. L. Standley and Nancy V. Burt (Boston: G. K. Hall & Co., 1988), 140.

25. James Melvin Washington, *Conversations with God: Two Centuries of Prayers by African Americans* (New York: HarperCollins, 1994), xlviii.

26. Baldwin interview with Jordan Elgrably and George Plimpton in *Conversations with James Baldwin*, 240.

27. Octavia E. Butler, "The Monophonic Response," in *Darkmatter: A Century of Speculative Fiction from the African Diaspora*, ed. Sheree R. Thomas (New York: Warner Books, 2000), 415.

28. Howard Thurman, *Disciplines of the Spirit* (1963; reprint, Richmond, Ind.: Friends United Press, 1977), 90.

29. Baldwin, *No Name*, 16.

30. Baldwin, *Blues for Mister Charlie*, 31–32.

31. Baldwin, *Go Tell It*, 90.

Afterword

1. Randall Kenan, *Walking on Water: Black American Lives at the Turn of the Twenty-first Century* (New York: Knopf, 1999), 3–4.

2. Baldwin interview with Goldstein in Troupe, *James Baldwin*, 185. See Derrick A. Bell's *And We Are Not Saved: The Elusive Quest for Racial Justice* (New York: Basic Books, 1987).

Bibliography

Works by James Baldwin

The Amen Corner. New York: Dial Press, 1968.

Another Country. New York: Dial Press, 1962.

"Autobiographical Notes." In *Notes of a Native Son.* Boston: Beacon Press, 1955.

"The Black Boy Looks at the White Boy." In *The Price of the Ticket: Collected Non-Fiction, 1948–1985.* New York: St. Martin's Press, 1985.

Blues for Mister Charlie. New York: Dial Press, 1964.

The Devil Finds Work: An Essay. New York: Dial Press, 1976.

"The Discovery of What It Means to Be an American." In *The Price of the Ticket: Collected Non-Fiction, 1948–1985.* New York: St. Martin's, 1985.

"Every Good-Bye Ain't Gone." In *The Price of the Ticket: Collected Non-Fiction, 1948–1985.* New York: St. Martin's Press, 1985.

"Everybody's Protest Novel." In *Notes of a Native Son.* Boston: Beacon Press, 1955.

The Evidence of Things Not Seen. New York: Henry Holt and Co., 1985.

The Fire Next Time. New York: Dell, 1963.

"A Fly in Buttermilk." In *Nobody Knows My Name: More Notes of a Native Son.* New York: Dial Press, 1961.

Giovanni's Room. New York: Dial Press, 1956.

Go Tell It on the Mountain. New York: Alfred A. Knopf, 1953.

Going to Meet the Man. New York: Dial Press, 1965.

"The Harlem Ghetto." In *Notes of a Native Son.* Boston: Beacon Press, 1955.

"Here Be Dragons." In *The Price of the Ticket: Collected Non-Fiction, 1948–1985.* New York: St. Martin's Press, 1985.

"History as Nightmare." In *James Baldwin: Collected Essays.* New York: Library of America, 1998.

If Beale Street Could Talk. New York: Dial Press, 1974.

"Introduction: The Price of the Ticket." In *The Price of the Ticket: Collected Non-Fiction, 1948–1985.* New York: St. Martin's Press, 1985.

Just Above My Head. New York: Dial Press, 1979.

"Many Thousands Gone." In *Notes of a Native Son.* Boston: Beacon Press, 1955.

Nobody Knows My Name: More Notes of a Native Son. New York: Dial Press, 1961.

"No Name in the Street." In *The Price of the Ticket: Collected Non-Fiction, 1948–1985*. New York: St. Martin's, 1985.

"Notes for a Hypothetical Novel." In *Nobody Knows My Name: More Notes of a Native Son*. New York: Dial Press, 1961.

Notes of a Native Son. Boston: Beacon Press, 1955.

"On Being 'White' . . . And Other Lies." In *Black on White: Black Writers on What It Means to Be White*, edited by David R. Roediger. New York: Schocken Books, 1998.

"The Outing." In *Going to Meet the Man*. New York: Dial Press, 1965.

"Preservation of Innocence." In *James Baldwin: Collected Essays*. New York: Library of America, 1998.

"Previous Condition." In *Going to Meet the Man*. New York: Dial Press, 1965.

The Price of the Ticket: Collected Non-Fiction, 1948–1985. New York: St. Martin's, 1985.

"Sonny's Blue." In *Going to Meet the Man*. New York: Dial Press, 1965.

Tell Me How Long the Train's Been Gone. New York: Dial Press, 1968.

"The Uses of the Blues: How a Uniquely American Art Form Relates to the Negro's Fight for His Rights." *Playboy* 11 (Jan. 1964).

"White Man's Guilt." In *The Price of the Ticket: Collected Non-Fiction, 1948–1985*. New York: St. Martin's Press, 1985.

"White Racism or World Community?" In *The Price of the Ticket: Collected Non-Fiction, 1948–1985*. New York: St. Martin's Press, 1985.

Interviews and Conversations with James Baldwin

Conversations with James Baldwin. Edited by Fred Standley and Louis H. Pratt. Jackson: Univ. Press of Mississippi, 1989.

A Dialogue: James Baldwin and Nikki Giovanni. Philadelphia: J. B. Lippincott, 1973.

"Go the Way Your Blood Beats: An Interview with James Baldwin." Richard Goldstein. *James Baldwin: The Legacy*, edited by Quincy Troupe, 173–85. New York: Touchstone/Simon & Schuster, 1989.

"An Interview with James Baldwin on Henry James." Interviewed by David Adams Leeming. *Henry James Review* 8 (fall 1986): 47–56.

A Rap on Race: Margaret Mead and James Baldwin. Philadelphia: J. B. Lippincott, 1971.

"Revolutionary Hope: A Conversation between James Baldwin and Audre Lorde." *Essence* 15 (Dec. 1984): 72–74.

Secondary Sources

Aanerud, Rebecca. "Now More Than Ever: James Baldwin and the Critique of White Liberalism." In *James Baldwin Now*, edited by Dwight A. McBride, 56–74. New York: New York Univ. Press, 1999.

Allen, Shirley S. "The Ironic Voice in Baldwin's *Go Tell It on the Mountain.*" In *James Baldwin: A Critical Evaluation*, edited by Therman B. O'Daniel, 30–37. Washington: Howard Univ. Press, 1981.

———. "Religion Symbolism and Psychic Reality in Baldwin's *Go Tell It on the Mountain.*" *College Language Association Journal* 19 (Dec. 1975): 173–99.

Bell, Charles. *Fifty Years in Chains*. 1837. Reprint, New York: Dover Publications, 1970.

Bell, George E. "The Dilemma of Love in *Go Tell It on the Mountain* and *Giovanni's Room.*" *College Language Association Journal* 17 (Mar. 1974): 397–406.

Burns, Thomas A., and J. Stephen Smith. "The Symbolism of Becoming in the Sunday Service of an Urban Black Holiness Church." *Anthropological Quarterly* 51.3 (July 1978).

Campbell, James. *Talking at the Gates: A Life of James Baldwin*. New York: Viking, 1991.

Champion, Ernest A. *Mr. Baldwin, I Presume: James Baldwin-Chinua Achebe, a Meeting of the Minds*. Lanham, Md.: Univ. Press of America, 1995.

Cohen, William A. "Liberalism, Libido, Liberation: Baldwin's *Another Country.*" *Genders* 12 (1991): 1–21.

Collier-Thomas, Bettye, ed. *Daughters of Thunder: Black Women Preachers and Their Sermons, 1850–1979*. San Francisco: Jossey-Bass Publishers, 1988.

Cone, Cecil W. *The Identity Crisis in Black Theology*. Nashville: African Methodist Episcopal Church, 1975.

Cone, James H. *Black Theology and Black Power*. New York: Seabury Press, 1969.

Creel, Margaret Washington. *"A Peculiar People": Slave Religion and Community-Culture among the Gullahs*. New York: New York Univ. Press, 1988.

Daniels, David. "The Cultural Renewal of Slave Religion: Charles Price Jones and the Emergence of the Holiness Movement in Mississippi." Ph.D. diss., Union Theological Seminary, New York, 1992.

Darsey, James. "Baldwin's Cosmopolitan Loneliness." In *James Baldwin Now*, edited by Dwight A. McBride, 187–207. New York: New York Univ. Press, 1999.

Davis, F. James. *Who Is Black? One Nation's Definition*. University Park: Pennsylvania State Univ. Press, 1991.

Dievler, James A. "Sexual Exiles: James Baldwin and *Another Country.*" In *James Baldwin Now*, edited by Dwight A. McBride, 161–83. New York: New York Univ. Press, 1999.

Du Bois, W. E. B. *Darkwater: Voices from Within the Veil*. New York: Harcourt, Brace and Howe, 1920.

Earl, Riggins R. *Dark Symbols, Obscure Signs: God, Self and Community in the Slave Mind*. Maryknoll, N.Y.: Orbis Books, 1993.

Eckman, Fern Marja. *The Furious Passage of James Baldwin*. New York: M. Evans & Co., 1966.

Edelman, Lee. "The Part for the (W)hole: Baldwin, Homophobia, and the Fantasmatics of Race." In *Homographesis: Essays in Gay Literary and Cultural Theory*, 42–75. New York: Routledge, 1994.

Fabre, Michel. "Fathers and Sons in James Baldwin's *Go Tell It on the Mountain*." In *James Baldwin: A Collection of Critical Essays*, edited by Kenneth Kinnamon. Englewood Cliffs, N.J.: Prentice-Hall, 1974.

Fredrickson, George M. *The Black Image in the White Mind*. Middletown, Conn.: Wesleyan Univ. Press, 1971.

Gibson, Donald B. "James Baldwin: The Political Anatomy of Space." In *James Baldwin: A Critical Evaluation*, edited by Therman B. O'Daniel. Washington, D.C.: Howard Univ. Press, 1981.

Giggie, John. "God's Long Journey: African Americans, Religion, and History in the Mississippi Delta, 1875–1915." Ph.D. diss., Princeton Univ., 1997.

Greenberg, Cheryl Lynn. *"Or Does It Explode?" Black Harlem in the Great Depression*. New York: Oxford Univ. Press, 1991.

Harris, Trudier. *Black Women in the Fiction of James Baldwin*. Knoxville: Univ. of Tennessee Press, 1985.

– – –. "The Eye as Weapon in *If Beale Street Could Talk*." *MELUS* 5:3 (1978): 62–64.

– – –, ed. *New Essays on* Go Tell It on the Mountain. New York: Cambridge Univ. Press, 1995.

Harvey, Paul. "'Those Untutored Masses': The Campaign for Respectability among White and Black Evangelicals in the American South, 1870–1930." *Journal of Religious History* 21 (Oct. 1997): 302–17.

Heyrman, Christine Leigh. *Southern Cross: The Beginnings of the Bible Belt*. New York: Knopf, 1997.

Higginbotham, Evelyn Brooks. *Righteous Discontent: The Women's Movement in the Black Baptist Church, 1880–1920*. Cambridge, Mass.: Harvard Univ. Press, 1993.

Hood, Robert E. *Begrimed and Black: Christian Traditions on Blacks and Blackness*. Minneapolis: Fortress Press, 1994.

Johnson, Clifton H., and A. P. Watson, eds. *God Struck Me Dead: Religious Conversion Experiences and Autobiographies of American Slaves*. Philadelphia: Pilgrim Press, 1969.

Johnson, William C. "'To Dance in the Ring of All Creation': Camp Meeting Revivalism and the Color Line, 1799–1825." Ph.D. diss., Univ. of California at Riverside, 1997.

Jones, William R. *Is God a White Racist?* Garden City, N.Y.: Anchor Press/ Doubleday, 1973.

– – –. "Theodicy: The Controlling Category for Black Theology." *Journal of Religious Thought* 30:1 (1973): 28–38.

Jordan, Winthrop D. *White over Black: American Attitudes toward the Negro: 1550–1812*. New York: Penguin, 1969.

Larsen, Nella. *Quicksand* and *Passing*. Edited by Deborah E. McDowell. New Brunswick, N.J.: Rutgers Univ. Press, 1986.

Leeming, David. *James Baldwin: A Biography*. New York: Henry Holt and Co., 1994.

Lincoln, C. Eric, and Lawrence H. Mamiya, *The Black Church in the African American Experience*. Durham: Duke Univ. Press, 1990.

Lynch, Michael F. "Beyond Guilt and Innocence: Redemptive Suffering and Love in Baldwin's *Another Country*." *Obsidian II: Black Literature in Review* 7.1–2 (1992): 1–18.

———. "Glimpse of the Hidden God: Dialectical Vision in Baldwin's *Go Tell It on the Mountain*." In *New Essays on Go Tell It on the Mountain*, edited by Trudier Harris. New York: Cambridge Univ. Press, 1995.

———. "Staying Out of the Temple: Baldwin, the African American Church, and *The Amen Corner*." In *Re-viewing James Baldwin: Things Not Seen*, edited by D. Quentin Miller. Philadelphia: Temple Univ. Press, 2000.

McBride, Dwight A., ed. *James Baldwin Now*. New York: New York Univ. Press, 1999.

Margolies, Edward. *Native Sons: A Critical Study of Twentieth-Century Negro American Authors*. New York: Lippincott, 1968.

Marks, Morton. "Uncovering Ritual Structures in Afro-American Music." In *Religious Movements in Contemporary America*, edited by Irving Zaretsky and Mark Leone. Princeton: Princeton Univ. Press, 1974.

Miller, D. Quentin, ed. *Re-Viewing James Baldwin: Evidence of Things Not Seen*. Philadelphia: Temple Univ. Press, 2000.

Murphy, Joseph M. "Black Religion and 'Black Magic': Prejudice and Projection in Images of African-Derived Religions." *Religion* 20 (1990): 323–37.

Nelson, Emmanuel. "Critical Deviance: Homophobia and the Reception of James Baldwin's Fiction." *Journal of American Culture* 14.3 (1991): 91–96.

———. "The Novels of James Baldwin: Struggles of Self-Acceptance." *Journal of American Culture* 8.4 (1985): 11–16.

Ohi, Kevin. "'I'm Not the Boy You Want': Sexuality, Race, and Thwarted Revelation in Baldwin's *Another Country*." *African American Review* 33:2 (1999): 261–81.

Olson, Barbara K. "'Come-to-Jesus Stuff' in James Baldwin's *Go Tell It on the Mountain* and *The Amen Corner*." *African American Review* 31:2 (1997): 295–301.

O'Neale, Sondra A. "Fathers, Gods, and Religion: Perceptions of Christianity and Ethnic Faith in James Baldwin." In *Critical Essays on James Baldwin*, edited by Fred L. Standley and Nancy V. Burt, 125–43. Boston: G. K. Hall, 1988.

Payne, Daniel Alexander. *Recollections of Seventy Years.* 1886. Reprint, New York: Arno Press and New York Times, 1969.

Pitts, Walter F. *Old Ship of Zion: The Afro-Baptist Ritual in the African Diaspora.* New York: Oxford Univ. Press, 1993.

Raboteau, Albert J. "The Black Experience in American Evangelicalism: The Meaning of Slavery." In *The Evangelical Tradition in America,* edited by Leonard Sweet. Macon, Ga.: Mercer Univ. Press, 1984.

— — —. *Slave Religion: The "Invisible Institution" in the Antebellum South.* New York: Oxford Univ. Press, 1978.

Reilly, John M. "Sonny's Blues: James Baldwin's Image of Black Community." In *James Baldwin: A Collection of Critical Essays,* edited by Kenneth Kinnamon. Englewood Cliffs, N.J.: Prentice Hall, 1974.

Roediger, David R. *The Wages of Whiteness: Race and the Making of the American Working Class.* London: Verso, 1991.

Ross, Marlon B. "White Fantasies of Desire: Baldwin and the Racial Identities of Sexuality." In *James Baldwin Now,* edited by Dwight A. McBride, 13–55. New York: New York Univ. Press, 1999.

Ruether, Rosemary. *Sexism and God-Talk: Toward a Feminist Theology.* Boston: Beacon Press, 1983.

Schnapp, Patrician Lorine. "The Liberation Theology of James Baldwin." Ph.D. diss., Bowling Green State Univ., 1987.

Scott, James C. *Domination and the Arts of Resistance: Hidden Transcripts.* New Haven: Yale Univ. Press, 1990.

Scott, Nathan A., Jr. "Judgment Marked by a Cellar: The American Negro Writer and the Dialectic of Despair." In *The Shapeless God: Essays on Modern Fiction,* edited by Harry J. Mooney Jr., and Thomas F. Staley, 139–69. Pittsburgh: Univ. of Pittsburgh Press, 1968.

Shephard, Eli. "Certain Beliefs and Superstitions." In *The Negro and His Folklore,* edited by Bruce Jackson. Austin: Univ. of Texas Press, 1969.

Sikora, Frank. *Until Justice Rolls Down: The Birmingham Church Bombing Case.* Tuscaloosa: Univ. of Alabama Press, 1991.

Smith, Theophus H. *Conjuring Culture: Biblical Formations of Black America.* New York: Oxford Univ. Press, 1994.

Stearn, Charles. *Narrative of Henry Box Brown.* Boston: Brown and Stearns, 1849.

Simawe, Saadi A. "What Is in a Sound? The Metaphysics and Politics of Music in *The Amen Corner.*" In *Re-Viewing James Baldwin: Things Not Seen,* edited D. Quentin Miller. Philadelphia: Temple Univ. Press, 2000.

Standley, Fred L. *"Go Tell It on the Mountain:* Religion as the Indirect Method of Indictment." In *Critical Essays on James Baldwin,* edited by Fred L. Standley and Nancy V. Burt, 188–94. Boston: G. K. Hall, 1988.

Taves, Ann. *Fits, Trances, and Visions: Experiencing Religion and Explaining Experience from Wesley to James.* Princeton, N.J.: Princeton Univ. Press, 1999.

— — —. "Knowing through the Body: Dissociative Religious Experience in the African-American and British-American Methodist Traditions." *Journal of Religion* 73:2 (1993): 200–222.

Tomlinson, Robert. "'Payin' One's Dues': Expatriation as Personal Experience and Paradigm in the Works of James Baldwin." *African American Review* 33:1 (1999): 135–48.

Troupe, Quincy. *James Baldwin: The Legacy.* New York: Simon & Schuster, 1981.

Turner, Victor. *From Ritual to Theatre: The Human Seriousness of Play.* New York: Performing Arts Journal Publications, 1982.

Van Heusen, Lawrence Lewis. "The Embodiment of Religious Meaning in the Works of James Baldwin." D.A. diss., State Univ. of New York at Albany, 1980.

Walker, Sheila S. *Ceremonial Spirit Possession in Africa and Afro-America: Forms, Meanings and Functional Significance for Individuals and Social Groups.* Leiden: E. J. Brill, 1972.

Walker, Willie Earl. "Prophetic Articulations: James Baldwin and the Racial Formation of the United States." Ph.D. diss., Princeton Univ., 1999.

Warren, Nagueyalti. "The Substance of Things Hoped For: Faith in *Go Tell It on the Mountain* and *Just Above My Head.*" *Obsidian II* 7 (spring–summer 1992): 19–32.

Washington, James M. "The Origins of Black Evangelicalism and the Ethical Function of Evangelical Cosmology." *Union Seminary Quarterly Review* 32 (winter 1977): 109.

Washington, Joseph R., Jr. *Anti-Blackness in English Religion, 1500–1800.* New York: Edwin Mellen Press, 1984.

Weatherby, William J. *James Baldwin: Artist on Fire.* New York: D. I. Fine, 1989.

West, Cornel. *Prophesy Deliverance! An Afro-American Revolutionary Christianity.* Philadelphia: Westminster Press, 1982.

Williams, Delores S. *Sisters of the Wilderness.* Maryknoll, N.Y.: Orbis Books, 1993.

Index

James Baldwin's God was designed and typeset on a Macintosh computer system using QuarkXPress software. The text was set in Adobe Cochin. This book was designed and typeset by Bill Adams and manufactured by Thomson-Shore, Inc.